Delivering Web Reference Services to Young People

**Walter Minkel
and
Roxanne Hsu Feldman**

AMERICAN LIBRARY ASSOCIATION
Chicago and London
1999

While extensive effort has gone into ensuring the reliability of information appearing in this book, the publisher makes no warranty, express or implied, on the accuracy or reliability of the information, and does not assume and hereby disclaims any liability to any person for any loss or damage caused by errors or omissions in this publication.

Trademarked names appear in the text of this book. Rather than identify or insert a trademark symbol at the appearance of each name, the authors and the American Library Association state that the names are used for editorial purposes exclusively, to the ultimate benefit of the owners of the trademarks. There is absolutely no intention of infringement on the rights of the trademark owners.

Project editor: Joan Grygel

Cover design: The Publishing Services Group

Text design: Dianne M. Rooney

Composition by the dotted i in Berkeley using QuarkXPress v. 3.32

Printed on 50-pound White Vellum, a pH-neutral stock, and bound in 10-point coated cover stock by McNaughton & Gunn

The paper used in this publication meets the minimum requirements of American National Standard for Information Sciences—Permanence of Paper for Printed Library Materials, ANSI Z39.48-1992. ∞

Library of Congress Cataloging-in-Publication Data

Minkel, Walter.
    Delivering Web reference services to young people / Walter Minkel
and Roxanne Hsu Feldman.
        p.   cm.
    Includes bibliographical references (p.   ) and index.
    ISBN 0-8389-0743-1
    1. Children's libraries—Reference services (Libraries)—United States—Data processing.   2. World Wide Web (Information retrieval system)   3. Library information networks—United States.   I. Feldman, Roxanne Hsu.   II. Title.
    Z674.75.W67M56   1998
    025.04—dc21   98-26112

Printed in the United States of America.

03   02   01   00   99   5   4   3   2   1

Contents

Figures

Preface

Metaphors for new technologies seem to appear whenever a new technology does; the classic example is the term "horseless carriage" for the automobile at the turn of the twentieth century. When the bulky portable video cameras that preceded camcorders first appeared, the media enthusiastically said that we would all become moviemakers. Of course, we all remember that, um, droll term "information superhighway" that was on so many people's lips when the Internet first entered public life. (Can you say "roadkill?") Since the World Wide Web became a trendy place to spend one's time, writers on the subject have compared it to many places and things.

If we must compare the Web to something, what should it be? One writer compared it to a library with all the books dumped on the floor. Another said it was like a million filing cabinets maintained by a thousand filing clerks, each of whom works for a different company, speaks a different language, and uses a different filing system.

We like to think of the Web as a flea market. Hundreds of people are displaying and selling things; some are original creations; others are obviously stolen goods. One booth features excellent, high-quality merchandise; the booth next door offers the cheapest kinds of imitations by no-name manufacturers. Some people are showing off their personal treasures; others are trying to make a fast buck any way they can. Then there are those people in the back who have set up those curtained booths (oops! aren't there a lot of holes in those curtains?) with the 25-cents-a-look signs. As we pass by, we need to mind all those protesters marching around them, trying to keep the kids in the crowd from peeking.

The Web is a flea market, and it's also a glorious mess, full of energy, controversy, and fun. If your job requires you to manage it and make it comprehensible to young people in a school or public library, we can hardly blame you if the words "mess" and "controversy" seem much more descriptive than others when dealing with the Web.

If you're a library staff member or volunteer who works with young people—particularly with students between the ages of 8 and 18—and you want to improve your skills at Web reference and training, please read on. If you stay with us, we aim to share with you

> what the Web does well for young people, and what it does poorly
>
> which Web skills are developmentally appropriate for which grades and ages of students

how to use search engines and subject directories to find what you and the students you serve want

how using your good old library catalog skills can, with a little bending, make you a whizzy searcher

why most young people, even those who use the Web a lot, are usually poor searchers

how to evaluate the sites you find on the Web

how to assemble the good sites into a subject directory or "webliography" for student, teacher, or library use

why creating a vital subject directory for your library (or linking to someone else's directory) can be great for your reference services

how to encourage staff, students, and volunteers to have fun with the Web

how having fun with the Web can improve young people's Web skills (and yours) ten times faster than a bunch of Help files and tutorials

We're going to assume a few things. (Yeah, we know what happens when you assume, but we're going to risk it.) We assume that you have or are about to get Web stations (that is, PCs with a browser installed that are hooked up by modem, T1 line, or otherwise, to the Internet) in your library that are accessible to you and your users. We assume that you have a rudimentary knowledge of at least one of the two primary browsers— Netscape Navigator or Microsoft Internet Explorer. In other words, you know what hyperlinks are and how to click on them; you know how to use the Back, Forward, and Stop buttons; and you know how to type a URL (Uniform Resource Locator or Web site address) into the Location box in your browser. If you would like an introduction to Navigator and Internet Explorer, see the Web sites in the "webliography" (a bibliography of Web sites). We also assume that you want to serve your young library users better by connecting them with the information they want and need, and you're willing to learn some new skills for a new medium.

This book is *not* a list of good sites on particular homework topics. There are plenty of those out there already, and listing sites is something the Web does better than books can; Web sites change every day. We mention several sites in the text, but by the time you're reading it, they may have vanished, substantially changed, or moved to another location.

You will find some URLs within the text; those not in the text are example sites listed in our webliography. If you want to be sure the list of sites is current, check our Web site at http://www.igloo-press.com/ WebReference/. You can even ask us questions, and we'll answer them if we can. The Web site contains our favorite links and examples as well as some samples you can use as starters for handouts in training sessions.

Many librarians who are receiving public Internet access for the first time are looking for ideas on how to train their users and how to set up policies for Web stations. We will offer links to sites that present this material as well as collect and present suggestions and training materials you send us, or we can link to such materials on your own site.

Acknowledgments

In appreciation, we would like to acknowledge the help of Elizabeth Overmyer of Berkeley (California) Public Library. Her well-reasoned comments, fact checking, and suggestions improved our work. We would also like to thank Susan S. Smith of the Bedford (Indiana) Public Library and Karen Ulric of the New York Public Library for the information they supplied.

1

How the Web Works and How It Doesn't

You've no doubt heard those who don't make their living in libraries ask whether books are on their way out now that the Net is here. Well, they thought that radio would disappear once television appeared on the scene, and they thought movies would die once VCRs became commonplace. So it goes behind our libraries' reference desks; the old media (books, periodicals, newspapers, audio cassettes, and microform) hang around while the new medium of the Net is added. We need to know them all.

How does the Net fit into reference work with young people? In some places it shines, and in other places it flops royally. Let's look at three typical K–12 student reference questions.

Example 1
The Current-Events Question

Picture yourself at the reference desk of your library (or standing in the middle of the floor, or at the circulation desk, or wherever you typically are when someone asks you a question). "On the radio this morning," a student says, "I heard these guys just broke the world land speed record in this rocket-powered car. There are these two teams that're trying to do it; one's American and one's British. Which one was it, and how fast?"

"Which team broke the record, do you mean, and what was their top speed?"

"Yeah."

If you were given this question, where would you look? The newspaper, of course, is what would come to mind first for most librarians. But what if you don't find it there—because it happened after the paper was put to bed—or what if someone's reading the paper when you get the question?

Events that are late-breaking and of worldwide interest, such as setting a new land speed record, are natural questions to answer using the World Wide Web. The CNN Web site will no doubt have a story, and so will several other news-media sites. The added advantage of these news Web sites is that they will probably have a color picture of the car, the winning team members, or both. In some cases the site will include a video file that the student could watch if your Web station is set up with appropriate plug-ins (computer programs that present the multimedia features on the Web).

EXAMPLE 2
The Science Experiment Question

You've also had the following question from third and fourth graders a dozen times over the years.

"Do you know how to build a model volcano?"

"A model volcano that erupts?"

"Yeah!"

Somewhere in that old card file, you have a note card with a citation for an old photocopied article that you hope hasn't been lifted from the pamphlet file. You know that the book that also had the answer was checked out just the day before.

Is there a better way than digging in the pamphlet file to answer this one? Well, yes, actually. The Volcano World Web site (see figure 1.1), housed on the North Dakota State University server at http://volcano.und.nodak.edu/, has complete instructions, with pictures, for building a model volcano.

EXAMPLE 3
The Poem That's Checked Out

Let's look at another reference example. This time it involves a poem that has been checked out.

A sixth grader comes up to you. "I need that poem," she says. "'Sarah Sylvia Cynthia Stout Would Not Take the Garbage Out.'"

"The poem by Shel Silverstein?"

"Yeah."

The book is checked out, so you look for it on one of the Web's search engines. You can quickly travel to several sites from which you can order the poet's recording of his work, but you can't find the full text that way, either. So you have to put *Where the Sidewalk Ends* on reserve for her.

Shel Silverstein isn't likely to give his poems away for free. There are some needs the Web can't meet—at least not for free—and supplying free copies of popular copyrighted material is one of them. However, if another student is looking for writings by nineteenth-century and earlier authors

Figure 1.1   Volcano World Web Site

Building Volcano Models

1. Paper and Cardboard Volcanoes: Shields and Stratovolcanoes
2. Three-dimensional Cardboard Volcanoes
3. Simple Clay Models
4. Explosive Volcano Model
5. Volcano Lava Recipe
6. Lava Flows on Plastic Three-dimensional Maps
7. The Poor Man's Pebble Volcano
8. The Electronic Volcano
9. Paper Volcano Model
10. Your Volcano Models
11. How Calderas and Craters Form

and poets such as Emily Dickinson, Edgar Allan Poe, Mark Twain, Oscar Wilde, or Lewis Carroll, that student is often in luck if the library has a Web station, even if all anthologies are checked out because of a class project. Many public domain materials are available online.

How can you guess when the Web might have an answer for a student question and when it's best to stick to the book or periodical collections or to borrowing material from another library?

The "State of the Web" (for Student Reference Questions, Anyway)

As we write, the Web is a *wonderful* place to find some things, such as

up-to-the-minute news

scientific information, particularly in astronomy, geology, paleontology, physics, chemistry, and the physical sciences in general (Although much of it is on a university level, there's quite a bit that isn't.)

entertainment and current fine and performing arts—anything from popular TV shows and movies to opera and ballet

medical, health, diet, and exercise information

sports and recreation

anything dealing with computers, technology, or the Internet itself

businesses and commercial products, but usually not the histories of businesses and commercial products (We once tried to help a fifth-grade student find material on the inventors of Coca-Cola and Life Savers candy, to no avail.)

certain ready-reference questions such as weather forecasts, currency conversion, feet-to-meters conversion, and calendars (such as lunar, various cultural, and old calendars)

It's a *satisfactory* place to find some other things. (In other words, you will often find incomplete information, or the information might be inappropriate for students or might be poorly organized.)

government and political information (There's lots of it on the Web, but it's often difficult to find the specific item you want, especially on a student level.)

material on young people's authors and illustrators (Some have their own sites, some have several sites, and many are barely mentioned. The size and detail of sites often do not coincide with the popularity or reputation of the authors.)

country or state information (Unless sorted beforehand, the travel-oriented material far outweighs the material suitable for student use.)

history and the social sciences in general (By far, the material in this area is on a university level, and K–12 material is hard to locate.)

multicultural material (Some cultures, such as Native Americans, are covered in many student-level sites; others, like Asian- or Latino-Americans, are not well-covered on a student level.)

Some topics are *poorly covered* on the Web on a student level. These include

biographical material (There are not many sites that cover the lives of individuals well—books still rule here.)

literature that is under copyright (for obvious reasons)

world religions and beliefs in sites that are not doctrinal

The problem in general isn't so much with the Web itself but with our expectations of it. The media have made it sound like the Web is this shiny, lively, well-organized Encyclopedia Universalia, in which all users can find exactly what they want in a matter of a few mouse clicks. How many of you have had a library user, friend, or relative come up to you and say, "Hey, how're you going to keep the library going and keep your job now that everything's on the Internet?"

Our response is always something like, "Well, the Net doesn't have everything. Usually it has the same stuff over and over in about twenty different forms, tons of stuff is missing, everything is really badly organized, and most people still need librarians to find what is there. So we're not worried yet."

Elizabeth Gerber, a library assistant at Virginia Commonwealth University's Tompkins–McCaw Library, told us that when teenagers come in to her library to do research for papers, they look upon Web searching as a challenge, even when they're not quite certain what they're doing. "Teenagers," she said, "are more willing to play around with the Web searching tools, and are ultimately more likely to find what they are looking for," even if they must spend a long time doing so. They often deny they need any help. "They are usually happy with me," Gerber said, "if I just get them started in our Internet search page and then cut them loose."

Adults, on the other hand, more frequently seem to have accepted the happy media messages about the ease of navigating the Web. Gerber finds that many adults "get very frustrated with Internet searching—quickly. They don't expect to have to go through their search results to find the right thing, and they often refuse to spend more than fifteen minutes digging on the Web. They come to me expecting a specific URL for their needs." So do many younger children, for whom the Web is an exciting but formless mess. (See the following section.) We have had experiences with parents who expect exactly that for their children's most-specific assignments.

Sound familiar to you? If so, you know that "a URL for every exact topic" is not exactly the way it works. You can find wonderful color pictures of anteaters or of the Great Wall of China without useful information about either. You'll see almost nothing about World War I, lots about the Civil War, and little about the history of Africa. Many sites about typical homework topics have so little content that there's little information that's usable for a report. Right now, using the Web requires sharpened evaluation and interpretation skills beyond the abilities of many students.

The Web and Developmental Appropriateness

Anyone who works with young people under twelve is probably familiar with a concept and a term that has come out of the early childhood education community: "developmentally appropriate practices" (DAPs). We probably think of DAPs only in reference to babies through first or second graders. However, the concept of developmental appropriateness applies to students of all ages, and it applies not only to craft projects and gross motor activities but to the proper use of high technology as well.

How do DAPs work? According to a Web page, "Developmentally Appropriate Practices: Right for All Kids," by Danielle Houser and Cathy Osborne at http://www.nauticom.net/www/cokids/dapei.html,

> Developmentally appropriate practices require teachers to make decisions in the classroom by combining their knowledge of child development with an understanding of the individual child to achieve desired and meaningful outcomes.

A growing number of librarians working with young people have been receiving training in developmentally appropriate practices, too.

Many of us feel that it will benefit our services to young people when we understand their developmental milestones and their skills and attention spans at particular ages. We can then better meet their informational and recreational reading needs (or, for younger children, their looking and listening needs) and their programming needs. We do not, for example, expect toddlers in a story time craft period to be able to cut with the children's scissors they'll be able to handle easily by the time they're four. We do not expect five-year-olds to be able to sit still for a forty-five-minute storytelling program that does not involve some fingerplays, stretches, and other activities that help them "work the wiggles out." We also do not expect a third-grader doing a report on China to read Lawson's *The Long March: China under Chairman Mao* and extract and interpret information for the assignment.

Those of us who have worked with children and computers know that much children's software of the kind that is currently available on CD-ROMs becomes attractive and usable to many children at an early age. We've seen children of two and three enchanted by and involved with KidPix or the Broderbund Living Books series. These programs, which require few or no reading skills, have been developed in ways that are developmentally appropriate to young children after they are shown once or twice how to move and click the mouse.

The Web is not so friendly to younger children—at least not yet—because it's slow, and it's overwhelmingly text-centered. There are a few sites that are suitable for preschool and K–1 kids, such as Sesame Street Central at http://www.ctw.org/sesame and Carlos' Interactive Coloring Book at http://www.ravenna.com/coloring/. However, the Web as a whole is so unstructured and so filled with text that it is nearly impossible for those who cannot yet read well (or read at all) to comprehend and use.

Even the two sites listed require an adult or older child to find the sites in a list of text links or from a bookmark to start them up. The designs of most Web sites are so different from each other that their structure is hard to learn when text-literacy skills aren't strong.

An even greater obstacle to young children is the sluggishness with which most pages (Web documents) load and the limited amount of multimedia (sounds, music, and animation) on the vast majority of pages. We have seen—frequently—younger children click on a Web page, wait for something to happen, wait a little longer, and then finally give up and go elsewhere before the page has completely loaded. TV and CD-ROM software have trained them to expect things on a screen to move much faster.

Sure, there's animation on many Web sites, but typically it does the same thing over and over and over in a small space, whether the child clicks on it or not. Even when a child is a good reader, there are still quirks and obstacles he or she has to learn to bypass. Many sites have banner ads that dance and flash yet have nothing to do with the content or purpose of the site. If the child clicks on them, he or she is carried away to an advertising site that has nothing to do with the original site. Such animations catch the eye in a way that's more distracting than involving. Young students can get lost and easily confused by being "whisked away" to a site that has nothing to do with their real query. For example, a third grader looking for material on ancient Egypt might find herself looking at a links page. At the top of the page, she might see the banner ad for an online solitaire game. The child, not realizing that the solitaire game has nothing to do with her search, clicks on the banner ad and finds herself at the Riddler's games site.

As absorbing as these animations can be for young children, they are of a much simpler order than the developmentally appropriate, cause-and-effect, full-screen animations of, say, the Living Books CD-ROM version of Tortoise and the Hare. Here the child clicks on different parts of the screen, and things happen in response to each click. Young children need to be able to manipulate things and to have those things respond in predictable ways when manipulated. Compared with such CD-ROM software, without quite a bit of adult intervention, Web pages simply aren't very interesting to most children under the age of eight or nine. Even for many fourth and fifth graders, long wait times can be detrimental to the usefulness of the Web. We've seen how slow many of the Web stations in public and school libraries can be, especially during the peak Net traffic hours of the school day.

A superficial interest in the Web can begin at an early age because children tend to be drawn to bright colors—and to monitors that look like TV sets. However, the ability to sustain interest even when the screen is blank and the capacity to discern content from advertisements require a certain mental maturity. For most young people, interest in the Web and what it offers doesn't really begin until the ages of ten through twelve. These ages are when most children have attained sufficient patience to wait for a page to load (most of the time, anyway). They have sufficient levels of literacy to read the text that is still the dominant mode of communication on the Web and to understand that they must spell search terms properly if they are to find sites on that topic. They also have some visual literacy—the ability to "read an image" well enough to click the correct buttons on a navigation bar and understand the significance of clicking a particular button to go to a certain page. There are exceptional younger children, and even classes of younger children guided by exceptional teachers, However, for most young people, fourth and fifth graders are typically ready to begin using the Web with guidance, and middle and high school ages are the times when the Web really becomes useful and interesting.

One of the baselines of developmentally appropriate practices, however, is to take into account the needs of the individual child, and this includes an individual young person's information needs. There are ways in which answering questions and showing students in second through fifth grades can make successful use of the Web. If a student wants color pictures of Jupiter's moon Europa (see figure 1.2), something that only appears in black and white in your books, or wants pictures of things

Figure 1.2   Sample Public Domain NASA Photo on the Web

Europa

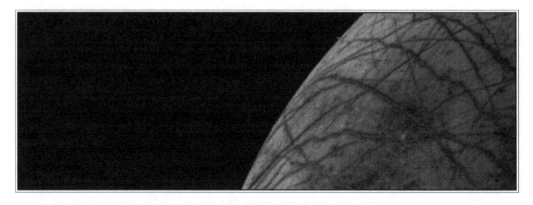

SOURCE: Photo of Europa found on Bill Arnett's "Nine Planets" site at http://seds.lpl.arizona.edu/nineplanets/nineplanets/europa.html. Reproduced with permission of Bill Arnett; Copyright 1994, 1995, 1996, 1997 by William A. Arnett.

like a catapult or a kind of medieval helmet you simply can't find in your books, the Web is often the perfect place to look, regardless of the student's age.

Showing the Web to younger questioners requires a good deal more handholding. If you are familiar with navigating the Web and—especially—if your library has created or is linked to a good subject directory of topics of interest to young people, you can easily demonstrate to the younger student where to go to find the answer. However, often even bright students below fourth grade will need you to stand behind them and coach them step by step until they're through for each new topic.

We know of a second-grade teacher who regularly goes onto the Web with her students to access a selection of animal and dinosaur sites. She shows the children how to navigate within the sites she's selected, and she remains nearby as they click on all the cool T-Rex, velociraptor, and dolphin pictures. However, a librarian often doesn't have the luxury of that kind of constant engagement with all students in a public library or a school setting. Sometimes when you're at the desk and people are waiting, you will simply do it all for the younger students, showing them what you're doing as you do it.

Do not expect students younger than middle school age to tackle more than the simplest uses of the Web. Even many students of high school age are poor searchers. Using a Web searching tool is a process that can be learned fairly easily, but it involves several other skills that a large number of students below the age of middle school don't have. These skills include the abilities to spell and type carefully, to compose a question or problem, to structure a pinpointed search, to interpret results, and to make value judgments from graphic clues. (This last skill is necessary to read and interpret Web directory annotations and searching tool hits pages.) Such skills are what many educators call "information literacy" skills (see the appendix). In the next two chapters we'll talk about these skills, but first let's look in greater detail at what subject directories and search engines are and how they work.

2

Using Search Tools
for Reference Work

One of the most confusing things about the Web, even for people with a lot of Web experience, is the use of search tools—search engines, subject directories, and metaengines. Plenty of these search tools are out there on the Web, but the tricks come in selecting the one to use for a particular search, constructing the search properly for a particular tool, and interpreting the results. Let's look at each kind of search tool, for without understanding how search tools work, performing reference service for young people on the Web will rarely be pleasant.

Definitions of Search Tools

First, let's define our terms and distinguish between the three major varieties of search tools. To explain the difference to librarians, we compare them to a user who comes to the reference desk asking where to find recipes.

Subject Directories   If the user comes to the desk and says, "I'm giving a dinner party Saturday, and I want to look at some interesting recipes. I've got nothing in particular in mind; I want to browse around." Typically, you would point this person in the direction of the 641s. For such people who want to explore a large topic area on the Web, a subject directory is a good choice. Yahoo is probably the best-known subject directory, the type of search tool that comes closest to being a library catalog. (See figure 2.1.) Subject directories are databases of Web sites sorted

Figure 2.1   Yahoo's Search Box

by human beings into indexes, by topic, that users can browse. There are search boxes in many subject directories, but they typically search only for sites in that particular directory. Subject directories are most useful as broad guides to a topic; use them if you want to browse a major subject area rather than do a finely pinpointed search. Because of the nature of its gathering process, the numbers of Web sites hosted on subject directories are often drastically smaller than those on other search tools.

Metaengines   Let's say that the person giving the dinner party comes to the desk and asks instead for Lebanese recipes. Obviously, browsing through the 641s isn't appropriate; you want to find resources that will appear in far fewer places. A metaengine—a cleverly written bit of software—is the tool appropriate to this kind of search. A metaengine is the place to go if you want to look for simple searches on small, but not pinpointed, topics. Metaengines are software programs accessed through Web sites that submit a search simultaneously to several "search engines"—software programs that accumulate databases of Web sites and allow access to these databases (see the following section). Because no single search engine can cover anything close to the entire Web, a good metaengine will sort the results of several search engines and rate the results for appropriateness. One of our favorite metaengines is MetaCrawler, which allows you to search AltaVista, Excite, Infoseek, Lycos, WebCrawler, and Yahoo at the same time. (See figure 2.2.) Other good metaengines are Inference Find and DogPile (one of the best names for a search tool we've seen).

Figure 2.2   MetaCrawler's Search Box

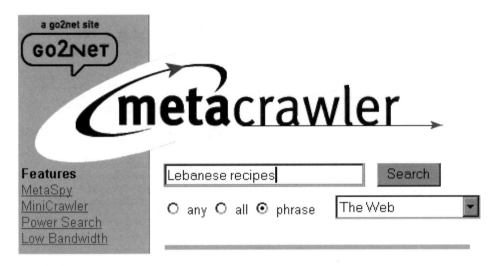

Search Engines   Now let's say that the user comes up to the desk and says, "I want to cook a Lebanese recipe for a dinner party on Saturday, and I want to use the eggplant I have on hand." The search has become very specific. You want to find Lebanese recipes, but only Lebanese recipes that contain eggplant. A full-featured search engine is the tool to use in this case; it will allow you to search for the phrase "Lebanese recipe" and to require that the word "eggplant" also appear on the page. The primary difference between a subject directory and a search engine proper is that search engines operate entirely through cleverly written software. Applications called "bots" or "spiders" traverse the Web daily, collecting text from thousands of Web sites and placing that text into enormous databases with little or no human intervention. Individuals can also submit their Web site URLs to the search engine to have the text added to the database. Unlike subject directories, users may not browse the search engine's database; all searches are done through typing keywords into a search box. AltaVista, HotBot (see figure 2.3), and Lycos are all search engines. The search engine is the place to go if you're looking for that Lebanese recipe with eggplant, but it is not a good place to browse through recipes in general. A search engine will dump ten thousand recipes in your lap in no particular order. Will you have time to look through them all?

Figure 2.3   HotBot's Search Box

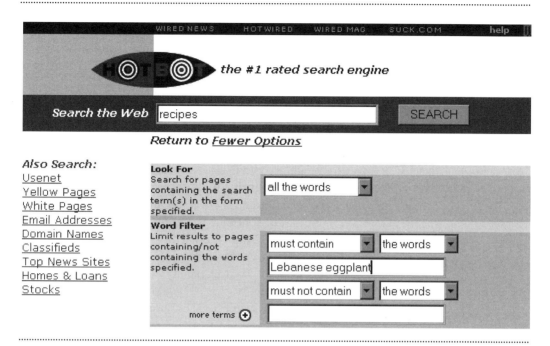

Planning Your Search

Before you begin working with search tools, however, it's important for you and the students you're helping to plan the search. As a librarian, you probably have a pretty good intuitive feel for which search terms might work in a catalog, but the search engine designers have no Library of Congress to guide them. The kinds of searches that work well in an automated catalog don't always work well in a search tool. Don't think you're going to get lost with a search tool, however; your searching experience puts you ahead of the vast majority of people fumbling around in Yahoo, Infoseek, or AltaVista.

The most important thing to know about search tools is to know when *not* to use them. Unless the question is one that is answered perfectly by the Web—for example, current news, metric conversion, or pictures of celebrities—keep the Web as a source of last resort. If you have a book or magazine or video on the topic the student needs, and that material will supply enough information, you don't need to use the Web. Searching for a site you're not certain exists is often a long and tedious process, and most librarians we know don't have that kind of time.

Searching Steps

Training students to search is an essential job for librarians. You must experiment with all types of search tools, read the help files, and develop your own "curriculum" when students begin fumbling. Here are our recommendations.

Analyze Your Topic

Before you touch your fingers to the keyboard, analyze your topic. What, exactly, are you looking for? What search terms should you use first? Young people searching impulsively for a map of the Battle of Gettysburg might type "civil war" into a search engine because their class is studying the Civil War, with results similar to those shown in figure 2.4—223,086 hits, most having nothing to do with the specific information being sought. (Don't laugh; we've seen it happen.) If you are looking for such a map, you will probably want to begin with all the words "Battle Gettysburg map."

Most search tools will not search for common words like *a, an, the, from, by,* and so forth, nor will they look for individual letters of the alphabet. So you should leave these out of your search unless you are searching for a phrase and putting a string of words in quotation marks, such as "Battle of Gettysburg."

Figure 2.4 Results of a Broad Search

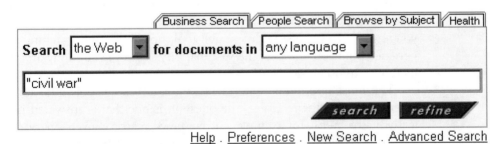

Choose Your Search Tool

Think about which search tool might be best to try first. Of course, you must be familiar with a search tool or two to know which to try. In the search, you might want to try the search engine HotBot's enhanced searching features because they will let you specify that the page for which you're looking must contain the exact phrase "Battle of Gettysburg," plus it must contain a "map." Note that in figure 2.5 the Image box is checked. This doesn't guarantee that you will get a map, but it does eliminate pages without images.

Figure 2.5   HotBot's Enhanced Searching Feature

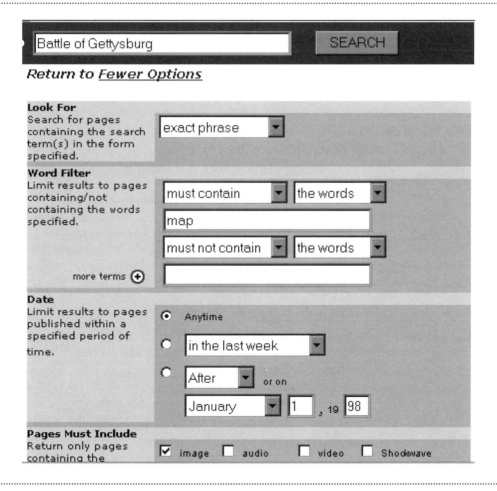

Change Search Terms

If a search doesn't work, change your search terms. If you get too many inappropriate hits, add a new search term that helps pinpoint your search or exclude a term that appears in many of the sites you don't want. If you get few or no hits, either change your search term to a synonym or begin removing words from your terms.

Rethink the Search

If you've chosen the right tool, and you still get no appropriate hits, think hard. Not everything is available on the Web, and a lot of what is available is highly academic, bureaucratic, or commercial. If you don't get an appropriate hit on the first hits page, you will need to rethink your search. Have you exhausted all the other material the library has?

Applying the Searching Steps

Let's go through two searches for typical questions and demonstrate the right way and the, well, *less* right way to do them.

EXAMPLE 1
Correctly Selecting Your Search Terms

We're going to do this search deliberately wrong to demonstrate what often happens when students are turned loose among the search tools. We'll try Yahoo first, because we find that students often go there first, whether it's appropriate to the search or not. Yahoo is constructed as a subject tree. Each topic branches into finer topics.

A fifth-grader comes up to the reference desk and says, "I need something on Mt. St. Helens."

"The volcano, you mean? For a science report?"

"Yeah."

We would imagine that a search for Mt. St. Helens would branch from science, to geology, to volcanoes, and finally to Mt. St. Helens. But it didn't. In Yahoo on January 27, 1998, the subject branches returned were

Society and Culture: Religion: Faiths and Practices: Christianity: Denominations and Sects: Catholicism: Churches. (This one led to church sites in the vicinity of the mountain.)

Two branched into Business and Economy: Companies: Travel:.

Another branched to Recreation: Outdoors: Camping.

The others were from Regional: U.S. States: Washington: and Regional: U.S. States: Oregon. All of these were sites for cities and businesses near the volcano. Excuse me, Yahoo, where were the branches for Science, Geology, and Volcanoes? There were none.

Next, still in Yahoo, we went into the subject tree itself, something novice searchers also often do. We clicked on Science, then Earth Sciences, then Geology and Geophysics, then Volcanology, and then typed "Mt. St. Helens" into the search box, asking Yahoo to search only in "Volcanology." The response we received:

Found 0 categories and 0 sites for Mt. St. Helens

We made faces at the screen when we saw that response.

Next we tried another trick.

If you have a multiword term that you feel strongly should be covered *somewhere* in a search tool, step back to the one word that you feel is most likely to bring you results.

We could imagine that the periods typed after "Mt" and "St" might have confused Yahoo, so we typed only "Helens" in the Volcanology search box.

Yes! This search did bring us useful results, and here is why—our search was constructed incorrectly *for Yahoo* from the beginning. The proper branch of the subject tree that contains the Mt. St. Helens links runs as follows:

Science: Earth Sciences: Geology and Geophysics: Volcanology:
Volcanoes: Mount St. Helens - Washington

Do you see the mistake, a mistake a young searcher could very likely make? To find the science sites in Yahoo on Mt. St. Helens, you must type "Mount." This search brought us three useful sites on the mountain and taught us the importance of thinking carefully of alternate search terms and of removing terms when they jinx a search.

Library Subject Directories

There are many other subject directories on the Web, many of which are created by or for libraries. The best example of a librarian-generated subject directory is The Librarians' Index to the Internet created by Carole Leita and housed on a server at the University of California Berkeley. (See figure 2.6.) This directory differs from Yahoo's in that it is nowhere near as large, and the search function is not as sophisticated. However, any site in the list has been selected for the quality of its content and its ease of use. Similar subject directories are those on the Internet Public Library site, the My Virtual Reference Desk site, and (covered in chapter 4) Multnomah County (Oregon) Library's Homework Center.

Figure 2.6 The Librarian's Index to the Internet Directory

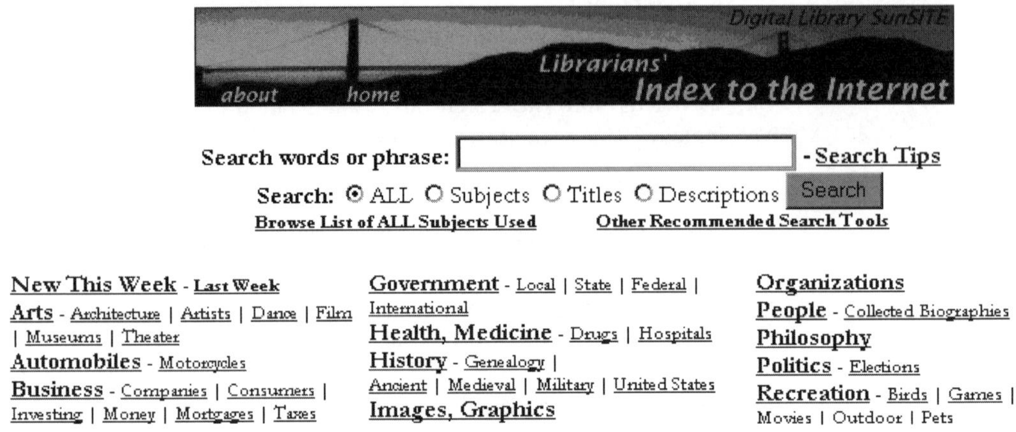

We tried "Mount St. Helens" and plain "Helens" in the search engine for The Librarians' Guide to the Internet, and the engine returned no links. However, typing "volcano" into the search engine did return three sites with information about Mount St. Helens.

EXAMPLE 2
Animal Reports—They're Tricky Beasts

One of the most common topics for Web reference is animals, partly because young people desire large quantities of material on often obscure species for animal reports—and the books on those species usually disappear quickly after the assignment is given. Let's look at a typical assignment and attack it the way an uninitiated person might.

Let's say a fifth grader comes up to you and says, "I need stuff on the red fox."

"Facts about the animal 'red fox,' you mean? For an animal report?"

"Yeah."

"About how many pages do you need to write? What do you need to know?"

"At least two." He pulls out an assignment sheet and shows it to you. "About habitat, size, range, what it eats, a picture of it, and whether it's endangered. I need three sources but not an encyclopedia."

A search of the shelves revealed one circulating book with a few paragraphs on the red fox and a page the student can photocopy from an animal reference book. For the third source, we tried the Web.

Searches for material for animal reports seem to be easy and straightforward. However, they often prove to be problematic, as you will see in the following example. Let's start, once again, in a subject directory, with Yahooligans. (*Warning:* this is, again, the wrong place to start. We really don't have a grudge against Yahoo and Yahooligans—we use them for some very general searches ourselves sometimes. But because Yahoo is the most-used search tool in the world as we write, we need to describe what we've seen happen with kids at the keyboard far too many times.)

We typed "red fox" into Yahooligans on November 4, 1997, and Yahooligans replied:

No match found for red fox.

Like the initial response from the Mount St. Helens search, we found this response hard to believe, so we tried Yahooligans again, going back a step to a more-general search term, "fox." This time we had no better luck.

Unlike a typical library catalog, in which you can define a search term as a topic, Yahoo and Yahooligans search by word only, not by topic.

For "fox," we received several hits on the Fox Valley Montessori School and several more on the Fox TV network but nothing on the animal fox. We also browsed the animals branch of the Yahooligans subject tree and found no sites on foxes.

Yahoo, Yahooligans, HotBot, and MetaCrawler returned almost all commercial business sites, like the one for the Red Fox Salsa Company, when we simply typed the words "red fox" into the search tool, specified exact phrase, and hit the search button.

Words such as common names for animals that are used for other purposes, like geographical and street names or in commercial products, make fuzzy, "messy" search terms.

Next we searched the way we should have from the beginning.

We tried HotBot, a search engine that allows very precise searches, and refined our search a little more, using the enhanced searching feature (see earlier example shown in figure 2.5). If you use a search engine regularly, take the time to learn its advanced capabilities, which can help you find the right hits in the smallest amount of time. HotBot's programmers change its "look and feel" regularly, but if you click on the "More Options" button, you're given many ways to pinpoint a search.

We wanted a page on the red fox that includes information on diet and habitat, so we typed in the main search box "red fox" and set the search-type menu to exact phrase. Then we went to the next box down and set up the search so that it must include the words "diet" and "habitat."

HotBot will also let you specify pages created or updated within certain dates as well as pages that include graphics files or files in other media, such as video.

> Our results from this search were far more encouraging. Numerous useful pages appeared on the screen of hits, including pages from zoos, universities, and elementary schools.

There is another way we recommend to search for animals and plants. If you would like to go directly to good-quality pages on any living thing, search in any search engine or metaengine. We have had good results using AltaVista, HotBot, and MetaCrawler by typing in the scientific name as a phrase. How do you find the scientific name quickly? Dictionaries, encyclopedias, and animal reference books usually can supply them. In the case of our "red fox" question, the animal reference book that served as the student's number 2 resource included it. You can also get the scientific name off the Web in many cases by visiting the Merriam-Webster site's dictionary at www.m-w.com/dictionary.htm and typing in the common name. When we did, it returned *Vulpes vulpes,* which we then placed in MetaCrawler as a phrase. The metaengine returned several worthwhile pages from zoos and wildlife parks with color pictures and all the information our student needed.

Searching for Images

An eternal reference question from children and adults alike is "Can you find me a picture of _____?" Answering this question has never been easy. If you've been doing reference work for any length of time, you know that the "perfect picture" to answer the question either does not exist or resides in a book or magazine you saw six months ago whose title you can't recall. The Web makes looking for images easier because it has so many graphics that are easy to print or save to a floppy disk.

A few good free sites for pictures are on the Web, and one of the best is the "Image Finder" page on the University of California Berkeley's Sunsite at http://sunsite.berkeley.edu/ImageFinder/. Here you'll find search boxes that allow you to search the UCB Sunsite's database of historical photographs of California, the Library of Congress's image databases of U.S. historical photographs (including some excellent Civil War photographs), the Smithsonian Institution's photo database, and several other graphics databases (some of which are more useful than others). All are searchable by keyword.

HotBot's More Search Options page, as mentioned previously, lets you search for "Images," although this feature works in a spotty fashion. To the search performed earlier for the exact phrase "red fox" that required the words "diet" and "habitat," for example, we added a check on the image button. True, this did lead to several pages with good pictures of the red fox, but it also led to other pages with images, like "Back to Home Page" graphics, that had nothing whatever to do with the red fox itself. Other images are cartoon graphics of fox characters. Imageseek, part of the Infoseek site, is also worth a look.

The search engine AltaVista will let you search for graphics as well by typing "image:[name of image]", but *think* before you type some words into an image search. If we go to the AltaVista search box and type "image:fox," for example, several of the images that will appear in the hits page will not be images of the animal "fox" but images that are more along the lines of "foxy babes." Likewise, never type the word "teen," "girl," or "woman" unless you want to see at least a few links to X-rated material. Whenever you search for "teen," "girl," or "woman," be certain you use qualifying words, for example, women in Philippine history. However, be aware that qualification isn't foolproof: we know of a librarian who searched for "girls and science" as a phrase and received a link to an "adult" site near the top of her first hits page. If you are easily embarrassed, do these kinds of searches when a student is not reading the screen over your shoulder.

The search engine Lycos has a "Pictures and Sounds" search page that allows you to click on the pictures button and type (in quotes, to specify an exact phrase) "red fox." Although many of the images returned in the hits page were not images of the animal, several good pictures of red foxes appeared.

For more information on graphics on the Web, see chapter 5.

More Searching Tips and Tricks (We've Got a Sackful)

Here are some more tips and ideas that don't fit into the examples we gave previously. They are bits of Web wisdom we've collected from several dozen of our colleagues, and we've found they're good to know.

Don't try to learn all the search engines and subject directories. Master two or three of them and don't worry about the others. Give yourself a question and try to find material using each search engine. Reading and memorizing the search Help or Tips file always available on each search tool's home page is crucial to developing your search-engine skills. You cannot take these help files—which we know many people ignore—lightly. If you cannot memorize all the tips, print them out and keep them close by for when you need to do a tightly focused search. HotBot and MetaCrawler offer more-helpful features, as search engines go. Yahoo and Yahooligans can be very useful when you have a clear idea of the path to your topic, but you may find another search tool better matches your personal style.

Learn the methods of Boolean searching.   Boolean searching is a logical way to fine-tune your searches. Take a look at the HotBot frequently asked questions (FAQ) on Boolean search terms at http://help.hotbot.com/ faq/advanced.html#sfeature10. There you'll get a simple description of how to use the basic Boolean operators and other search terms: *AND* or the ampersand *&, OR* or | (pipe), *NOT* or an exclamation point *!*, open and closed parentheses ( ), and quotation marks "". Some of these terms are used in more-complex queries than you'll typically need for homework questions.

Let's look at some Boolean expressions you might find handy. We will continue the "red fox" example to demonstrate the use of Boolean operators in HotBot:

If you type

"red fox" AND diet AND habitat

you are constructing a Boolean search. The quotation marks here signal to the search program to look for "red fox" as an exact phrase (a term and not two separate and unrelated words). The term *AND* is just that: AND— meaning all three terms "red fox," diet, and habitat—*must* be present in the document returned. This way, you have about 200 files returned and many of them will have at least some appropriate information on the animal "red fox."

If you type

"red fox" AND (diet OR habitat)

you are constructing a different Boolean query. You are telling the search program to look for "red fox" as a phrase, but the document can contain "red fox *and* diet" or "red fox *and* habitat." or "red fox *and* diet *and* habitat." With this search you'll retrieve about 1,300 documents.

If you type

"red fox" AND habitat NOT diet

then the search program will look for "red fox" and "habitat" in a document and will *exclude* any file with the word "diet" in it. This way, you retrieve about 900 documents.

Lycos offers even more in-depth search strategies if you choose to use the Lycos Pro option. You can specify the *relationship* between your query words—NEAR, ADJACENT, FAR, and BEFORE to make the search even more precise.

In the AltaVista advance search, you have to use the symbols for the operators. Thus "red fox" & diet & habitat returns about 150 documents; "red fox" & (diet | habitat) returns about 900 documents; and "red fox" & habitat & ! diet—AltaVista does not accept simply NOT argument, it has to be AND NOT—will return about 650 documents.

Most search tools allow the following searching concepts.

+ meaning "must have"
− meaning "must NOT have"
~ meaning "near"

To be certain what search operators are allowed, check the tool's Help file.

Be aware that some kinds of searches don't work in most search engines.   For example, we were helping a bright middle school student who wanted to find sites about the C programming language. A great many programming sites exist on the Web, yet nothing would come up in HotBot because most search tools will not let you search for a single letter, even when it's part of a phrase like "C++ programming." Infoseek's Ultraseek engine, however, will let you search for single letters, punctuation marks, or common words like "and," "to," and "new" in phrases that are necessary for particular searches.

Check your spelling and phrasing.   Most young people in our experience are not very good typists, so remind them to check carefully what they type into the search box, just as they need to check carefully what they type into the library catalog. Several libraries help by keeping paperback dictionaries near the Web stations. Be particularly careful typing scientific names and non-English words, for they are particularly likely to slip past you before you click on that Search button.

How you phrase your search is important, too. If you are searching for information on German shepherds, it is better to type "German shepherd" (as a phrase, of course) because most tools will find more sites if the phrase or word you type is singular. If you are searching for sites on Santa Fe, New Mexico, remember to include all four words for the place name. If you type only "Santa Fe" as a phrase, you will get a lot of railroad sites and advertising sites. Similarly, don't even think about typing "china" into a search box without some qualifying terms if you're interested in finding sites on porcelain or gravy boats.

Remind young users that the library's catalog is a search tool, too. There are plenty of times when a book is both the best choice and easier to find than a Web site. Sometimes the Web dazzles the eyes of young people and they have trouble seeing that the catalog is there.

Which Tool to Use for What and When

When do you use each search tool? Following are some recommended tools for each search objective.

Survey of a Topic or a Broad Overview

For an overview of a topic, use one of the commercial subject directories like Yahoo, Yahooligans, or Magellan because they let you browse by topic. Excite has a browsable database in addition to its search engine. Serendipity works wonders on the Web, sometimes, much as it does when you browse a library shelf. Don't forget the many library subject directories out there (see chapter 4). Do not use HotBot, AltaVista, or Infoseek search engines for a broad overview kind of search; they will bring you hundreds of thousands of hits on some broad topics.

"Simple" Search Using a Well-Chosen Word or Phrase

Metaengines will compare and rank your searches from different engines to give you the most likely hits using a single-term or single-phrase search. For a simple search—one that can be expressed in a phrase such as "Scarlet Letter" or "Battle of Gettysburg," a metaengine, like Meta-Crawler or Inference Find, will be the most helpful because it will search several search tools simultaneously.

Pinpointed Search for Very Specific Information

Do not use Yahoo or one of the large subject directories for a pinpointed search. Also, do not use a metaengine for doing pinpointed searches in which you want to include or exclude certain additional search terms or request graphics, video, or sound files. Search engines handle each of these kinds of searches differently.

For a search in which you want to use Boolean search terms, to require or exclude certain search terms in addition to a phrase, or to search for specific media types (graphics, sound files, or video), use a search engine like HotBot, AltaVista, or Infoseek. These tools let you use features that allow searching within specific dates, for specific media formats, language, or continent of the world.

Sites Chosen for Quality and Utility   Magellan has a small database of sites rated for quality and suitability for young people ("green light sites"). In addition, The Librarians' Index to the Internet has a small database of high-quality sites for use in library reference, although the "Kids" section is quite small. Furthermore, the ALA 700+ Great Sites has approximately 800 quality sites chosen by children's librarians. Also, a list of "Homework Help" sites around North America is given in the webliography for this book.

Image, Sound, or Video File   Use Ultraseek's Imageseek, HotBot's Supersearch, or Lycos media search. AltaVista will also let you specify a search for images.

Home Page of a Corporation, Nonprofit Organization, or School   You may find a page deep in the site you desire on a search tool's hits page instead of the home page. Why is this so? Who knows? It happens frequently, though. Click on that page's URL, and when it comes up in your browser, delete everything in the URL *except* for the string directly after the http:// and before the single slash. In searching for the New York Public Library site, you might find http://www.nypl.org/branch/kids/people.html among the hits. Delete everything after .org and you will reach the New York Public Library home page.

Particular Domain Type (.com, .edu, or .gov)   MetaCrawler and Hot-Bot Supersearch will let you specify the domain type. (Domains are explained more fully in chapter 3.) We have been asked several times, "Is there a way to look at everything but .com sites?" Sorry, no. You should be aware that many of the best information sites are in the .com domain. Take a look at www.nationalgeographic.com if you don't believe us.

Particular Person   Most search tools will find individuals fairly easily if the sites exist and the names are not too common. Be aware, for example, that most university sites worldwide contain enormous lists of that institution's faculty and students. We would not want to look for sites on the nineteenth-century antislavery activist John Brown unless we used HotBot's "More Options" and required the phrase "Harpers Ferry" to appear as well. HotBot will also retrieve pages that include the name in "either direction"—both Brown, John (inverted) and John Brown.

Person's, Association's, or Business's E-Mail Address or Telephone Number   There are several fairly good phone and e-mail directory sites. Among them are WhoWhere (see figure 2.7), Switchboard, and BigYellow. See the webliography for a list of finding people and/or businesses sites.

Lyrics to Songs   Try the International Lyrics Server. You'll find lyrics to more than 70,000 songs, including current hits and old traditional songs. Note that you'll find the lyrics only, though, not the music. There is some question about whether the International Lyrics Server, which is located in Switzerland, is in fact complying with copyright law. The individual song lyrics appear to be typed up by volunteers from unnamed sources and no individual copyright notices are placed on the pages of lyrics. The page says that "If a user makes a request for, or later uses, a photocopy or reproduction for purposes in excess of 'fair use,' that user may be liable for copyright infringement." It does *not* say whether placing the lyrics on the server in the first place violates copyright.

Figure 2.7   WhoWhere Search Screen

Material in a Particular Field or Language   Several directories of sites concentrate in specific areas. Planet K–12 can be a handy search tool for education-oriented sites. CNET's "search.com" directory is a Yahoo-like collection of sites that can bring you information from specific fields with an emphasis on the commercial, such as travel and careers. If and when you have free time, examine sites in various topic areas. Remember, for example, that travel sites can give you information on holidays worldwide and common phrases in the world's languages. AltaVista provides an English translation of pages in other languages. From what we hear, the translations are passable, but we can expect this technology to improve.

Search Engines and Commercials

We librarians pride ourselves on our objectivity, but many of us secretly wish in our heart of hearts that the search tools we use daily were "objective" and uninfluenced by commercial motives. We know they're not; they have financial agendas (and rightly so for the growth of their companies and services). Please, as you work with search tools and teach others how to use them, keep in mind that all the search tools that end in ".com" are businesses. (See chapter 3 for more information on URLs.) If we were all paying Yahoo and AltaVista for their services the way we pay our circulation system vendors, we could have a commercial-free environment. The goal of commercial search tool companies is to make money, as much of it as they can, and they usually do that through selling ads and cementing corporate partnerships. How they do these things affects the way these tools look and operate.

There isn't necessarily anything bad about the search engines we use for reference work being so blatantly commercial, but we should remember that as long as we depend on "free" search engines to do our searching, we, and the kids, will have ads in our faces. When we teach the kids how to use the search tools and the ads pop up before the search box does, we smile and tell them, "It's just like a TV show; the commercial comes first." We point out the ads to young people when it seems appropriate, and we remind them, "These may look cool, but they're only ads; they usually don't have anything to do with the stuff you're looking for."

Northern Light, one of the newer search engines, has created a niche for itself in the search tool market. It has licensed access to databases of articles from periodicals and journals and sells full-text copies of these articles for $1 to $4 each, while giving access to Web sites for free. See figure 2.8 for Northern Light's home page. Such services are as yet rare.

Figure 2.8   Northern Light's Search Page

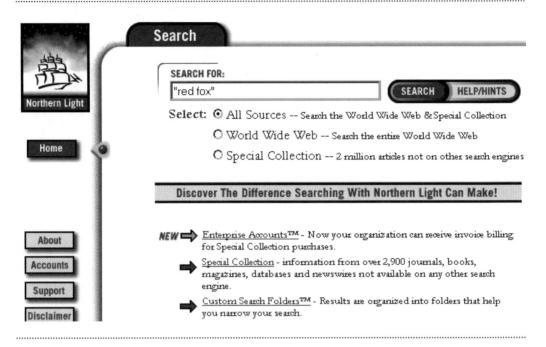

It's more common for the commercial search tools to set up "virtual shopping malls" (Lycos has one of these), news and stocks services, and similar features. Some commercial partnerships are easy to spot; others are subtler.

Infoseek, for example, the third-most-popular search tool at present, has a "Kids & Family Channel" that may be of interest to some of your users. Disney sponsors this section. If you look closely at the page and check out the links, you will see many references and links to Disney movies, the DisneyBlast subscription Web site for kids, and other Disney products. Lycos features links to Barnes & Noble and UPS within an inch or two of its search box, and Yahoo's site displays the VISA logo and a link to a "Visa shopping guide." AltaVista features links to amazon.com for any topic you are searching and attracts you to that online bookstore.

Using all your professional searching skills, you've finally found some sites with information that appears to be worthy of further inspection. How do you tell if any of these sites can be trusted as sources for student assignments? The following chapter provides some guidance on evaluating Web sites.

3

How to Evaluate Web Sites

School librarian Ann Symons has written in *School Library Journal,*

> The amount of useless content on the Web boggles the imagination. If you've spent even one day surfing the Net, it's obvious that you would never select more than one percent of what's on the Web for your print collection.[1]

We agree; structuring a search to find appropriate information instead of empty fluff or advertisements takes some thought.

However, once you or the students you're assisting find something on the Web that looks as if it might be useful, how can you (or they) be sure that the site you find is legitimate and accurate? Unlike the world of book and magazine publication, in which there are familiar names that suggest at least some kind of fact checking and quality control, anyone can put anything they like up on the Web. You and the students you assist need to gain and to sharpen your multimedia evaluation skills, skills that we often hear called aspects of "information literacy."

What Is Information Literacy?

In this age of electronic media, there are a growing number of educators who are lobbying for information literacy training for students.

> Resource-based learning requires that students are effective users of information regardless of format. Print resources such as books and magazines as well as electronic resources such as computer databases

29

and laser videodiscs will be used by students. Students will master information literacy skills when teachers and library media specialists guide them as they use information with a discipline or through an interdisciplinary project.[2]

Information literacy skills are not the skills to evaluate and use only what's on the Web. They also include the ability to read, view, listen to, comprehend, analyze, and make use of any medium—books, periodicals, maps, illustrations, videotapes, audiotapes, and computer software. Educators and corporate marketers have increased their attention in the last ten years to information "design," with a special emphasis on the visual display of information. Think for a moment about all the charts and graphs in *USA Today;* about the maps, graphs, and photos in the TV weather forecast; and about the spreadsheet software in most offices that allows users to put numerical data into sophisticated graphs.

Bellingham (Washington) School District's online Information Literacy and the Net course tells us of the need for visual literacy in our end-of-the-century culture.

> In a society where powerful interests employ visual data to persuade (what Alvin Toffler calls "info-tactics"), schools must show students how to look beyond the surface to understand deeper levels of meaning and tactics employed to sway their thinking.[3]

The Information Literacy on the Net curriculum takes students through six steps.

Questioning   What problem needs solving?

Planning   Where might the best information lie?

Gathering   If the planning has proceeded well, the time on the Net may be limited by direct hits produced by careful selection of good information sites.

Sorting   The student sorts and sifts the information much as a fishing boat must cull the harvest brought to the surface in a net. The student is looking for information that contributes to understanding.

Synthesizing   The student arranges and rearranges the information fragments until patterns and some kind of picture begin to emerge.

Evaluating   Questioning intensifies and leads to planning and more gathering. After several cycles, if the picture is reasonably complete, the evaluation stage suggests an end to the research cycle. It then becomes time for the reporting and sharing of insights—a related but somewhat separate stage.[4]

For more information on information literacy, check out also the American Association of School Librarians' Position Statement on Information Literacy in the Appendix. It is also available on the Web at http://www.ala.org/aasl/positions/PS_infolit.html. The position statement gives examples of how evaluating and understanding information in all its forms has become essential to the mission of the school librarian.

Information Literacy and Nontraditional Media

Information literacy training assumes that students will be using print and nonprint media. Nonprint resources are increasingly important at all levels in education as the twentieth century becomes the twenty-first. When asked for material to support a homework assignment, anyone working today at the reference desk of any well-supplied library can often find items in print, audio-visual, and electronic formats to answer typical questions, whereas twenty-five years ago almost everything in a typical library was in print format. Often students ask specifically for particular media, and many of us who help middle and high school students are familiar with students asking for a classic (and assigned) novel on tape or a movie version of the assigned Shakespeare play on video. Librarians need to feel comfortable with training young people to evaluate these kinds of nonprint resources.

The Web is only the newest of these media and still the least familiar of nontraditional formats to many students, teachers, and librarians. It's an amalgam of text, graphics, sound, and motion. The skills involved in evaluating Web sites differ somewhat from evaluation skills in all these other formats for several reasons. The most important of these is that Web sites do not always clearly identify who has produced them, nor do they always cite an authority for their content. Because "publishing" a Web site is far cheaper and easier than printing a thousand copies of a book or writing ten thousand CDs, there are far more "self-published" Web sites than publications in any other medium. As we often tell classes who come to the library for instruction, anyone with some kind of computer access—whether it's their own computer or someone else's—can put up a Web site. Many companies out there, like GeoCities or Tripod, are willing to give several megabytes of free server space to anyone who signs up for a free e-mail account (and who is willing to look at a lot of ads). None of these people, unless they want to make the effort for their own satisfaction, are required to make certain that what they put on their site is accurate.

Web sites also typically change over time—or they don't, while the information on a particular topic has changed eleven or twelve times. No other medium we've worked with as librarians has had the property of changing from day to day. Although a newspaper comes out with a new issue each day, the previous day's issue can be archived. In contrast, the CNN site might change every few hours on a busy news day. Much of the CNN site's articles might not be archived, so something a student finds today without using it as a resource might have disappeared when he or she needs it next time. A reliable source on the Web can also disappear (or be moved to another URL) without any warning. Librarians and students must acknowledge and learn to deal with the nature of the Web.

Web Site Evaluation Questions

Students often know *some* aspects of operating a computer quite well and other aspects barely, if at all. Most young people who have spent more than two or three minutes around a computer can navigate the Web fairly easily, and most know the minimal basics of how to type a search term or phrase into a search tool, for example. However, they're often uncertain about what to do when the hits screen appears. They may click through each of the first ten hits, waiting for each page and its graphics to load, hoping to find exactly what they're looking for. Yet once they arrive at a site, they'll spend only a few seconds looking at it; if they don't see instantly what they want, they're off, clicking their way to the next hit.

Unlike young students, librarians know very well how to navigate information sources like tables of contents, indexes, graphs, maps, and tables. We know how to select alternative search terms and put those search terms together for pinpointed searches. We know the basic types of reference resources and how to use them. All these skills, and this knowledge, still apply to what we do in the world online. They are basic skills that will serve in all areas of information literacy: the skills to evaluate illustrations, video files, and the printed or electronic word. We need to share these skills in a way that students who need to find things but don't want to make a career out of finding things can understand them. How do we look at a site and tell whether it's worthwhile?

Reviews of content sites are available both on the Web and in various library publications such as *Library Journal* and *School Library Journal*. However, there are still relatively few reviews and so many sites that need reviewing. Because many sites move and change over a period of a few weeks or months, a review you see one month may be inaccurate the next. There are also plenty of "cool sites" Web sites and print articles in mass-market periodicals, but these tend to focus more on the quirky or fluffy fun sites than the content-rich information sites. Everyone who does research or helps others find research materials must learn to turn print evaluation skills into site evaluation skills to avoid feeling swamped in words and graphics in this time of crazy change.

Following are questions every librarian and every student should have at hand when he or she goes onto the Web. These are expressions of the skills all of us received as we passed through school and the skills we learned on the job.

Is the information I want in the site? Can I find it if it is?

First, of course, you or the student you're assisting will look over the site to see whether it has the information needed. It helps if, as in the research process steps listed previously, the student has spent at least a few moments figuring out exactly what question or problem lies before him or her.

How quickly you or the student find that information usually depends on how well the site has been designed. An example of a masterfully done information site is Bill Arnett's "The Nine Planets," a multimedia tour of the solar system at http://seds.lpl.arizona.edu/nineplanets/nineplanets/nineplanets.html. As in a book, there is a table of contents on the first page with a list of all the astronomical bodies—planets, moons, comets—of the solar system. (See figure 3.1.) Unlike a book, all a student has to do is click on a topic in the list to find the kind of basic information he or she needs for an astronomy report. It's easy, clear, and fast, and there are no loud backgrounds or flashing graphics.

The Internet Public Library's POTUS (Presidents of the United States) at http://www.ipl.org/ref/POTUS/ is another good example of an easy-to-comprehend and easy-to-use site. Robert S. Summers, who created the site for IPL, did so with students who had to write a report on a specific President in mind. The site presents a menu of links to information on each president in chronological order. He also supplied an alphabetical index to names, titles, and subjects.

Unfortunately, there are many other sites out there that obfuscate their data. Unskilled Web designers will bury their links in the middle of long blocks of text that must be read before students can make their choices, or they'll give several levels of outline to click through, each requiring a separate page to load, before you can find the information you're seeking. Often sites like these have good information, but the more difficult they are to use, the less likely students are to stick around long enough to find it. For extremely lengthy text files, remind students to use

Figure 3.1 Nine Planets Contents Page

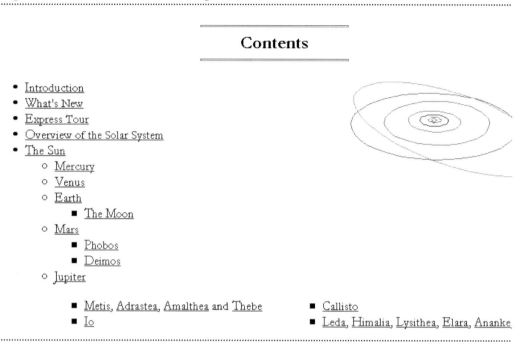

Contents

- Introduction
- What's New
- Express Tour
- Overview of the Solar System
- The Sun
  - Mercury
  - Venus
  - Earth
    - The Moon
  - Mars
    - Phobos
    - Deimos
  - Jupiter

- Metis, Adrastea, Amalthea and Thebe
- Io

- Callisto
- Leda, Himalia, Lysithea, Elara, Ananke

the Find button to search for the topic, word, or phrase that might lead to a fruitful read.

If you've helped a student with a search tool, you have probably experienced the following frustration: You've found what looked like a good hit on the desired topic. Then you've traveled to the page and found that the page has only three lines of information on the subject—and the student needs enough information to write a three-page report. Of course, the same thing happens with books, sometimes. Right now, however, many people's expectations of the Internet are higher than they are for books.

Other sites have some good information but have goals very different from supplying information to students for homework assignments. There are innumerable pages about the countries, cities, and natural wonders of the world that have been published by travel companies. They contain lots of information about hotels and tours but only bits of the historical and cultural information students need, or they break it up into chunks that must be read carefully and reassembled. U.S. government documents often house wonderful nuggets about endangered animals and Native American nations, but they are buried in masses of adult-level bureaucratic detail. While helping students, you should acknowledge to them that finding things on the Web isn't often easy. Encourage them not to bound off immediately to the next hit, but to examine pages carefully for those bits of valuable information they can incorporate into their assignments.

Is the content accurate? Are the spelling and grammar correct?

When you read the content in a site, check it against what you already know and what you can verify from other sources. Is a source given for the content? Whether we like it or not, many content site creators give no source for the information in their sites, and verifying that content against the materials in our collections, when possible (if you have the time), is one way to tell if a site is worth "keeping." Some site content is the creator's or sponsoring organization's opinion, pure and simple, particularly if a site deals with a controversial (and frequently researched) topic like animal rights, abortion, or capital punishment. Controversial topics typically find homes in many places on the Web, so encourage students researching them to look for an array of opinions. It also isn't difficult to find articles in the full-text periodical databases on controversial topics.

The spelling and grammar of the site's text is a good indicator of the time and attention the creator lavished on the site, or didn't.

Who put up the site?

Once you've located a page that looks promising, the next thing to settle is to determine who put it up there. Students should look at the URL first to get a hint. When giving a student training in Web site evaluation, we like to bring home the notion of the server-client relationship upon which the Internet is based.

We first remind students that a Web site is really a collection of files—HTML (hypertext markup language) files, graphics files, and so on—housed in a directory on a host computer, or server. Typing a URL into a browser (the copy of Netscape Navigator or Microsoft Internet Explorer you're using) tells the browser to request that particular set of files from that server, whether it's here in town or on the other side of the planet. Reading a URL often tells a lot about a site, particularly where, geographically and institutionally, that server might be. The following section is a quick analysis of URLs.

URLs Unraveled

URL stands for Uniform Resource Locator, which is a fancy way of saying "an address on the Internet." Some Web site URLs contain *www* (World Wide Web, of course) and others don't; it's the name of a particular Web server. Every Web site address begins with http, which stands for hypertext transfer protocol. Servers that provide other kinds of Internet information-retrieval methods, such as gophers (collections of plain-text documents) and ftp (software and document download services) sites, also have URLs, but their URLs begin with gopher:// and ftp://.

Every URL describes a path to a specific server—a computer wired to the Net that will send the pages of the site when you ask for them by clicking on a link or typing the URL in a Web browser's Open Location box.

When you see a URL, pay particular attention to the first segment after the http://; this is the site's domain name, and in many cases it will tell you a lot about the site.

http://www.nba.com

http://www.nike.com

Sites that end in *.com*—and this includes more sites than any other kind of domain—are commercial (business/company) sites. Most companies try to keep their URLs as short as possible to make them easy to type in and use, thus attracting customers. The companies for the previous two URLs are the National Basketball Association and Nike.

http://astro.uchicago.edu/adler/

A site whose domain ends in *.edu* is almost always a college or university site. The previous URL for the Adler Planetarium and Astronomy Museum is housed on a server at the University of Chicago. Notice the *uchicago.edu*. Sometimes you can tell at what university the site's server is located, but unless you know, for example, that *uiuc.edu* stands for University of Illinois at Urbana–Champaign, usually you can't. We can guess that the Adler Planetarium site is on the University of Chicago's astronomy department's server, which is named astro.

Here are other things you might see in a URL. You will notice below that we say "often" and "typically" a lot. This is because for every type of Web address, there are both general rules and a few exceptions.

www.pbs.org

www.unicef.org

The final part of the URL, *.org*, means the site is sponsored by a non-profit organization, such as the Boy Scouts of America, National Public Radio, Public Broadcasting System, United Nations Children's Fund, etc.

www.interport.net
www.att.net

The *.net* in the URL means that the site originates from an Internet-related business, usually an Internet service provider, Web site design business, or Net consulting service.

www.twingroves.district96.k12.il.us
http://magnet.temple.k12.tx.us

When you see *k12,* it means the site originates from a K–12 school district or sometimes a K–12 private school.

A tilde (~) in the address typically means that the site is a personal site, even if it is on a university or commercial server. Students and faculty of a university are often given server space, and subscribers to an ISP (an Internet service provider such as Netcom, Tripod, or GeoCities) often receive several megabytes of server space with their membership, but that doesn't mean that the university or the ISP sponsors those sites. America Online member sites do not contain tildes; instead the domain is http://members.aol.com/[name]/. Some other Internet service providers use "members" in their domain name as well. When you see the tilde, or "members," in a URL, be a little more cautious in accepting everything you see in a site as authoritative.

www.whitehouse.gov
ocls.lib.fl.us

The preceding are samples of phrases you will see in many American state and local government site URLs (in this case the Orange County Library System in the Orlando, Florida, area and the White House in Washington, D.C.).

When you see *.gov,* that means the U.S. government or another nation's government. Sites originating in various countries of the world often have their own two-letter abbreviations in place of the .us.

Canada	.ca	Italy	.it
Finland	.fi	Japan	.jp
France	.fr	Singapore	.sg
Germany	.de	South Africa	.za
Great Britain	.uk	Sweden	.se
Hong Kong	.hk	Taiwan	.tw

Note that .ca stands for Canada only if it isn't followed by a .us; if it is, .ca means California.

English seems to be very nearly the universal language of the Net, and pages in non-English-speaking nations often come with English versions. Therefore, don't be surprised when a page from a German or Finnish server appears in English.

When you're trying to remember a URL to type into a browser, be aware that some browsers will assume that you want to go to a commercial (.com) site. Many people, barraged by URLs in advertisements, think all Web addresses end in .com. If you are not trying to reach a commercial site, however, interesting things sometimes happen because site managers who are less than reputable, or those hoping to get hits from those who type frequently visited Web addresses into their browsers incorrectly, will use misleading domain names. There was a case in one library not too long ago in which a user typed www.nasa.com, looking for the NASA site, into a browser and reached a page with links to "adult" material. Many people are familiar with the White House Web site at www.whitehouse.gov, but if you type in www.whitehouse.net, you will reach a counterfeit satirical White House Web site put up as an ad by a Web-design firm. It looks very much like the real thing, so be aware. There also is another "adult" site at www.whitehouse.com.

Why is the site on the Web? Who is its creator or sponsor? What does its creator or sponsor want it to accomplish?

Look for the creator's or the sponsoring organization's name, and look for a way to contact the creator or sponsor if a student has a question or comment about the site.

One of the ways—but not the only way—you can tell that a site's creators or Web managers take responsibility for the content and currency of their site is that they make clear the purpose of the site. Many educational sites state their purposes right on their home pages, and many organizations with Web sites state the missions of their organizations and supply enough information about their organizations and their sponsors for site visitors to make evaluative judgments about the site. Supplying this kind of information is particularly useful if the creator of the site or the sponsoring organization is not well-known.

A good example of an informational site maintained by an individual is Bruce Hallman's "History of the Northwest Coast" at http://www.hallman.org/indian/.www.html. Although the URL includes .org, it is clear that this site is a part of Hallman's personal page, and the presentation is an expression of Hallman's personal enthusiasm for the topic. This site is about the Native American nations of the Northwest Coast. It is quirky, but it does include some excellent photographs and quotes from primary sources.

A good example of an informational site maintained by an organization is the Nemours Foundation KidsHealth site at http://www.kidshealth.org/

index2.html. There are three parts to this site—one for kids, one for parents, and one for professionals. The kids' section, despite some graphics that make the site look a little like its target audience is preschoolers, has an excellent selection of basic articles on health for older elementary and middle school ages.

Look for an e-mail link somewhere on all informational sites to the site's manager or creator so site visitors can make comments or ask questions about the site or the material in it. Look also for a street address or phone number for organizations. These are typically listed at the bottom of a site's home page. If an organization you've never heard of doesn't give a street address, there is a fairly good chance it's operating out of someone's den or garage. Not that there's anything wrong with that, but if an organization with no street address claims that George Washington was really an alien from Venus, a student should look for verification in a source a teacher would consider reliable before writing it in a history paper.

Does the site "work"?

The site should operate cleanly, provide what you need to know, and require no "puzzling out" from you (unless you're on a puzzle site). When you bring up the site in your browser, how quickly does it load? If a site takes more time than the typical time for your PC to load, it may suffer from too many large graphics, sound, or animation files. A conscientious Web designer should test how quickly a page loads over a 28.8 modem and a previous version of Navigator or Internet Explorer as well as the newest and fastest. Are graphics missing? When you click on links on the site, how often do you see "This page doesn't exist" or "404—Error"? As content on the Internet moves slowly toward more and more sound, video, and animation, it's important that a particular site work on your browser. Does the site tell you when you need a Java-capable browser or when you need to download "plug-in" files (see chapter 5) to view or hear multimedia?

On a more-basic level, is the text readable? Is it black text on a clean, light background, or is it yellow text on a bright red background? The color choices may give you a hint about how much the creator of the site cares about sharing the information on the site.

When was the site last updated?

A responsible Web manager will post, typically at either the top or bottom of a contents page, a "last updated" statement. This date lets users know when information or links were last added, corrected, or removed from a site or a page. It is a Web manager's professional duty to check all links regularly and respond quickly when site visitors report a dead link or one that needs to be changed. (Web managers can run a page through a link checker easily; see chapter 4.) Sites move and vanish on a daily basis, or disappear and then reappear at the same URL a few days later; a responsible site manager builds maintenance into a site's plan of operation. See figure 3.2 as an example of Web site update information.

Figure 3.2   Web Site Update Information

....

American Library Association
For questions or comments, contact ALSC.
www.ala.org/alsc/newbery.html
Last revised February 1998.
Copyright © 1998 by American Library Association.

....

Topics that are dependent on current information (such as sites dealing with ongoing scientific research or the political/social situations in various countries of the world) must be updated on a regular basis. If you see a page in your Web perambulations that has not been kept up, has dead links, or reflects the state of the topic in 1995, you should send the site manager a message, asking when the site will be updated.

Analyzing a Site

Let's evaluate a site that might appear on a search tool hits page. For our example, we'll use The History Place's American Revolution site at http://www.historyplace.com/unitedstates/revolution/index.html.

Is the content accurate, and is there enough of it? How about spelling and grammar? The History Place has supplied a very nice six-part time line of the American Revolution (see figure 3.3) with links to source documents from the time of the Revolution, sometimes with illustrations (as in the announcement of the Declaration of Independence shown in figure 3.4). Although no source is given for the information, we checked several random facts in a reputable reference book, and they were accurate. While these few pages are certainly not a full-length history of the Revolution, they do supply quite a bit of historically accurate information, including features such as the full text of the Declaration of Independence. It would serve well as an overview of the Revolutionary War for middle school or high school students. The spelling and grammar were correct. This site has obviously had a lot of attention, checking, and proofreading.

Who put the site up? It appears to have been put up by a business called "The History Place." We checked the site's home page for information about the company—whether it's affiliated with another better-

Figure 3.3   The History Place's Main Index Page

known corporation, where it's located, and who is the CEO—and found nothing. Only the following information is given: "Established July 4, 1996—Dedicated to Students, Educators, and all who enjoy History!" There is a "Recommended by the History Channel" seal near the bottom of the home page.

Why is the site on the Web? The History Place is obviously a business, selling and renting history videos from Reel.com, books from Amazon.com, and other history curriculum materials to teachers, but the content-to-advertising ratio on this site is good. The content is the reason to come to the site and, maybe, to check out the products offered, and there's nothing wrong with that as long as the content and ads are separate. There are links that lead to ads, but the ad portion of the site is clearly an ad, and the content portion is not.

Is there a way to contact the site manager/creator? Yes, there is, from an e-mail link at the bottom of the home page.

Does the site "work"? When we tested it, yes. All the links worked, and there were no unexpected surprises. The pages loaded fast, and the information was arranged in an orderly way, making it easy to find specific information.

Figure 3.4 Sample Illustration from The History Place

SOURCE: Copyright 1998 The History Place; reproduced with permission.

When was the site last updated? This is unclear. There is no "last up-dated" date on the site that we could find. For a history site that doesn't cover current events, updating is less of an immediate concern than it might be with other topics, but we would feel a little more comfortable if a last-updated date were supplied. (Especially if the site contains links to related sites, an updated links list may prove to be useful.) If updating is a concern, a student could send a message to the site manager, asking when a page was last updated. (We tested the address when we wrote the site manager to obtain permission to duplicate a page from the site in this book, and we received a reply within a few days.)

Webliographies as Offshoots
of Web-Site Evaluations

A Webliography has broad implications for libraries. Multnomah County (Oregon) Library School Corps, a public library school-outreach program, has for a while been creating webliographies on curriculum-related topics for teachers in county schools as part of its services. These usually take the form of bookmarks or fliers prepared using preset templates in Microsoft Word. Typical topics are career areas (marketing, physician's assistants and related health careers, or physical education careers), science (endangered species, regional wildflowers and trees, or space flight), and history (United States colonial crafts, Native American tribes of the Northwest, or explorers).

Each site is formally cited: its title and URL and an annotation. If you are interested in assembling a webliography, you don't even need to type to compile it. Annotations can sometimes be copied from the introduction to the site itself and pasted directly into your word processor, as can each title and URL. If necessary, a larger topic can be broken into subtopics. School Corps members select sites for appropriateness to the assignment and the grade level. The five School Corps members generate between ten and a dozen such webliographies monthly; each list takes between two and four hours' work to compile. See figure 3.5 for a short sample of the Multnomah biomes webliography.

While it would be unrealistic to expect a busy librarian to reserve big blocks of time to compile webliographies, such lists can be useful in the same way a library's printed book lists are useful. Once you have found and evaluated Web sites for reference work, you may decide to add them to your Navigator bookmark file or your Internet Explorer favorites list. Lists of sites on specific topics may also be useful for those "big assignments" that always flood over your ref desk like tsunamis several times a year and wash away all your books on their topics. They're also good as parts of cooperative work projects with particular teachers and classes. No matter who you compile them for, you can photocopy them and keep them on file for teachers and students asking you for materials for similar assignments.

If you've done your job in finding and evaluating Web sites that meet your reference needs, what do you do with all those good sites you've found? If you're like many librarians, you've assembled a long bookmarks or favorites file on your PC. Will this help when there are multiple Web stations in your library or when librarians in other agencies or school buildings would like to have them handy, too? Read on to find the answers to these questions.

Figure 3.5   Sample Webliography

BIOMES OF THE WORLD WEBLIOGRAPHY

<u>General Biomes Sites</u>

Marlborough's Biomes Page
http://www.marlborough.la.ca.us/depts/science/biomes.html
Links to sites related to world's biomes. Many of the links are to Sierra Club or EMAN (Ecological Monitoring and Assessment Network) which provide detailed summaries of characteristics of each biome.

The World's Biomes
http://www.ucmp.berkeley.edu/glossary/gloss5/biome/index.html
Created by the "Biomes Group" in a biology class at UC Berkeley. Presents detailed information for the Alpine, Aquatic, Grassland, Tundra, Desert and Forest biomes. Good for high-school level research. Each biome site is prefaced by a large example photograph of that particular biome.

United States Biomes
http://admin.aces.k12.ct.us/classweb/oxford/
Good overview of the United States biomes created by a sixth-grade science class. The indigenous plants and animals of each biome as well as the "ecological concerns" for each are discussed.

<u>Specific Biome Sites</u>

CHAPARRAL

Plant Biology 100 Lecture Notes (University of Maryland)
http://www.inform.umd.edu/PBIO/PBIO/pbio42a.html
This is a section of a lecture on biomes. The main focus is North America, but there is lots of information. *Note: some of the links within the text require a subscription to Britannica Online.*

Source: Created by Vailey Oehlke, Multnomah County Library School Corps, for Gresham/Barlow High School, Gresham, Oregon, 11/97.

Notes

1. Symons, Ann, "The Smart Web Primer, Part 2: Sizing Up Sites: How to Judge What You Find on the Web," *School Library Journal Online,* 1 Apr. 1997. Online. Available http://www.bookwire.com/SLJ/articles.article$3577.

2. American Association of School Librarians, "Position Statement on Information Literacy: A Position Paper on Information Problem Solving, 1996." Online. Available http://www.ala.org/aasl/positions/PS_infolit.html.

3. Bellingham (Wash.) School District, "Bellingham Schools Course Outline: Information Literacy and the Net," 23 Oct. 1996. Online. Available http://www.bham.wednet.edu/vislit.htm#visual.

4. Bellingham School District, "Course Outline."

4

Designing Your Homework Reference Site

Public and school libraries around the world are adding directories of "homework sites" (or "kids' sites") to their Web sites, and this is good. However, most of those homework site directories are not very complete or usable, and this is not good. A library's site is its face to the online world at large, and a small jumble of links on a page with no information besides a list of names in hypertext does not show a professional face. (See figure 4.1; this is not a real library Web site, but it is typical.) Note that the Web site contains no annotations, no URLs, and no alphabetization.

Dealing with the Web is a task many library staff members do not see as being as important as maintaining the "hard" collection. Yes, the Web is a fluid medium; the messages electrons bear are often ephemeral. A Web site may not contain the same quality and amount of content as a reference book. However, for many young people who are more comfortable with a keyboard under their fingers than their noses in a book, your collection of links to Web sites is essential and should be given as much attention and care as your book collection.

When we teach students how to find resources on the Web, we don't take them first to a search engine like Infoseek or a subject directory such as Yahoo. We show them our library home page first and how to get from there to our homework directory. "A lot of people," we tell them, "think that a library is this big room full of books and that's it. Well, that's not all of it anymore. Just like our book collection and our videotape collection and our magazine collection, we also have a collection of Web sites. We pick out the ones that are going to give you the best answers, and the great thing about this collection is that you can get to it from any computer with an Internet connection."

Figure 4.1 Poor Example of a Library's Homework Site

Astronomy Websites

<u>NASA</u>
<u>Project Galileo</u>
<u>Ask An Astronaut</u>
<u>Live From Mars</u>
<u>Star Child</u>
<u>Star Journey</u>
<u>Space Zone</u>
<u>Space Science Hotlist</u>

We warn students that the Web is not as good as the entire library and that the Web doesn't have everything the library has. "But if you can't get to the library, or it's closed," we tell them, "the library is still here, online, 24 hours a day to help you. When even our homework directory doesn't have what you need, that's when it's time to pull up Infoseek or Yahoo."

A good homework directory can be an incredible reference tool if it's planned, built, and maintained correctly. You need to give the selection of sites as much attention as you give to selection of books or periodicals. In fact, you must often give it more attention because so many of the sites you'll evaluate are created by individuals who aren't professional publishers and who do not see their audience the way you do. An example:

There was a library that, during the winter holidays one year, put up a page of links to various winter holiday sites. Presenting temporary sites for events or particular times of the year is something at which the Web excels, so that was great. There were links for Christmas, Hanukkah, Kwanzaa, the winter solstice, and a few other December holidays. So far so good.

One large Christmas site for both adults and children was assembled by a private individual. The site had a little bit of everything—lyrics to common Christmas carols, pictures for children to color, and classic Christmas poems and stories. This person had obviously put a lot of time and attention into the site. However, among the site's list of topics was Christmas humor, and this section, which was more "adult" than the others, had some of those classic tongue-in-cheek satires on "The Twelve Days of Christmas" in which, for example, the four calling birds are let go because the boss has seen their phone bill. There were also a couple of take-offs on "The Night before Christmas," and one of them was, um, quite sexually graphic. We sent a message to the librarian at that library, warning her about this site, and she was grateful (and we're sure, at least a little embarrassed) to learn about this one poem that did not fit the selection standard of a family-friendly collection. Thus, she pulled the site from her list of family holiday links.

The moral is that you must select your sites carefully and then go back and check them periodically to make certain they haven't changed in nature. If a site on your list is large, you need to look at every page and every section. This one poem was easy to miss.

Making Sense of the Web for Your Users

It is an important function of libraries serving users of all age levels and with all needs to make sense of the Web—to collect electronic Net sites, organize them, catalog them, and present them. Consultant and author Stephen Toub writes that "For patrons, the value of having their library provide access to remote Internet resources lies in the ways librarians add value to an Internet collection."[1] He states that librarians add value in two ways. They ensure "the findability of Internet resources via well-planned organization, navigation, labeling and learning systems," and they select, evaluate, and describe the resources in the collection carefully.[2]

Until very recently, there was little interest on the part of most media specialists and children's and YA librarians in compiling collections of Web sites for their young users. This was probably true because there simply weren't many Net terminals available for young people's use—or for the use of the staff people who worked with young people in libraries. The year 1997 saw a boom in the number of Net terminals available in public library children's areas and in school libraries. It also saw a boom in the creation of youth-oriented Web-site collections on school and public library sites and sites created by consultants and universities intended for use by students and young library users. Subject directories like The Awesome Library (http://www.neat-schoolhouse.org/awesome.html), Blue Web'n (http://www.kn.pacbell.com/wired/bluewebn/), and ALA's 700+ Great Sites (http://www.ala.org/parentspage/greatsites/) appeared during that year to fill the gap.

However, none of these sites is truly comprehensive, partly because the resources available on the Web don't yet cover all of the specific information needs of young people. As noted in previous chapters, the Web is not yet a reliable source of student-level information on many topics. We can anticipate that within a few years, a collection of cataloged links to Web sites will become a viable commercial product for libraries. We also expect that as Web-based catalogs become the rule rather than the exception. Web sites will be cataloged and will come up in author, title, and subject catalog searches the way "fixed" media such as books and audiotapes do now. Web-based catalogs will, of course, allow users to click on a link to access Web sites directly from catalog screens. However, such comprehensive technologies are not yet ready to find homes in most libraries. Software and features are still being developed. The line between information and sales on many sites is too blurry for many librarians to feel comfortable about selecting and cataloging them. Many librarians' unfamiliarity with and uneasiness about the loosey-goosey nature of the Web as well as the lack of enough search stations with browsers in many libraries make a difference.

Until that "something better" technology comes to your library, it's up to you to make as complete a collection of links to useful sites available to your young users as you can for homework and recreation. It's not difficult, but it will definitely be labor-intensive if you want to build a truly high-quality directory of links. The following sections outline the process of designing a young people's Web-reference collection. (Hereafter we refer to it as a "YPWRC," and by a collection for "young people," we mean a collection for users anywhere between ages five and eighteen.)

Deciding to Create a YPWRC

A recent discussion on the PUBYAC listserv for children's and YA library staff demonstrated that many librarians keep extensive bookmark files on the Net stations they use for reference. In these lists are the sites librarians use over and over to answer young people's, parents', and teachers' questions. We are frankly curious why, if the big bookmark file is such a prevalent feature among so many reference librarians, these librarians don't get together and create a page of links that can be accessed by all Net stations in the system or in the region. Creating a single page of frequently used "good sites" that are broken into a few simple categories and alphabetized is not that difficult and makes for a page that is easily shared with colleagues and users. Topics in demand at one library are usually in demand everywhere over a region or system—and everywhere else, for that matter.

Every library serving young people, no matter what its size or staffing, should have at hand a collection of links to Web resources that are available at all its Web stations. Based on experience and on discussions with librarians who make Web resources available to young users, we believe that every library should have a homework directory available to its users. This does not mean, however, that every library needs to create and maintain one. There are plenty of good YPWRCs out there, and they're easy to access. Alongside your links to some good YPWRCs, you should make a page of your bookmark collection. These are those sites that, in particular, meet *your* reference needs as well as those of your community.

Following are examples of two library homework directories that we feel are superior: the National Cathedral School (Washington, D.C.) Internet Directory and the Multnomah County Library (Portland, Oregon) Homework Center. Also highlighted is Kathy Schrock's Guide for Educators, a site for teachers that was created by a librarian. The librarians in charge each spent six months of hard work to create these resources and spend between two and four hours a week adding to and maintaining them. If you feel you have too little time to devote to assembling a YPWRC, talk to other librarians who use the Web regularly to answer reference questions. Ask them if they would be interested in working with you to compile one.

Do not try creating a YPWRC if you are not excited by or interested in the Web. We have seen, in our virtual perambulations, more than a few rudimentary YPWRCs filled with dead links, with "last updated" dates a year old or more, and with only a few unsorted links. It is better to link to a good YPWRC elsewhere if you and your library aren't ready to commit to doing the best job you can creating and maintaining your own. Even if you are very interested in helping your users explore the Web and feel that you can handle things yourself, you'll be better off if you are part of a committee. It's good to have others nearby with whom you can discuss site design, organization, and selection, for example, "Should I add this games site or not? The games are fun, but it has a lot of advertising." A library may involve the entire reference staff in hunting and evaluating sites, although one or two need to coordinate Web collection development. A few more people will make setting up the directory and maintaining it simpler.

If you are not feeling committed to developing a YPWRC but see the need to have a local links directory, ask around in your area and find a library in the region that has already created a good one. Ask permission to link to it. Typically, this library will be a larger public system, a statewide partnership or library cooperative, or a school district. An example from New York State is the Nassau County Libraries' site, a cooperative of more than fifty libraries. The NassauNet Kids Page (see the webliography) has a nicely annotated homework help directory of sites arranged by broad Dewey categories.

A new high-quality library subject directory is KidsClick, http://sunsite. berkeley.edu/KidsClick!/, created under a federal Library Services and

Technology Act (LSTA) grant obtained by the Ramapo Catskill (New York) Library System. Using the ALA Great Sites as its basis, the creators have added both a search engine and a growing number of appropriate sites with full URLs and annotations.

We do not recommend that you link *only* to one of the large national kids/homework site collections, like B. J. Pinchbeck's Homework Helper (http://tristate.pgh.net/~pinch13/), the ALA 700+ Great Sites (cited earlier), or the Internet Public Library (see the webliography). Such sites are fine for general homework help, but each region of the United States and Canada studies its own history and culture, and sites of local and regional interest are often missing from these general sites. Large local library systems and school districts in your area probably have compiled pages with sites of local and regional interest. Following are three examples to get you started.

Multnomah County (Oregon) Library Homework Center
http://www.multnomah.lib.or.us/lib/homework/

The Multnomah site contains more than a thousand Web sites that are sorted and are assigned subject headings. (See figure 4.2.) Being involved

Figure 4.2   Multnomah County Library's Homework Center Index Page

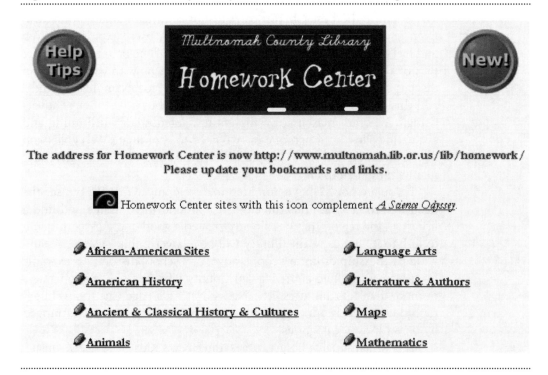

in this site, we're biased, but it exemplifies the philosophy of YPWRC construction we're promoting in this book. (See "How to Build a YPWRC" in a following section.)

The Homework Center grew out of a few homework help pages on Multnomah County Library's KidsPage, but one of the system's librarians, Kate Houston, took the help pages, mixed them with a list of bookmarks she'd saved, and created something big. As an example, take a look at the Homework Center's page of links on states. (See figure 4.3.) All students in the United States have to write at least one report on a state some time during their years between fourth and eighth grade, right? If they do, and they have access to the Web, they can't find information much faster than they will on the states information page. Kate has taken several large "megasites," as she calls them, like the Internet Public Library's "Stately Knowledge," and broken each one down, state by state, to allow students to go directly to the pages on the state they're writing about. There are also large pages on animals (including endangered species), historical topics, and scientific disciplines.

Kate and the other librarians on Multnomah County Library's "School Corps" school outreach program collect sites by asking the teachers what they're assigning. One of the School Corps' functions is to create bibliographies and webliographies for teachers in grades K–12. As they col-

Figure 4.3   Multnomah County Library's Homework Center States Page

State Report Information

- Alabama
- Alaska
- Arizona
- Arkansas
- California
- Colorado
- Connecticut
- Delaware
- Florida
- Georgia
- Hawaii
- Idaho
- Iowa

- Illinois
- Indiana
- Kansas
- Kentucky
- Louisiana
- Maine
- Maryland
- Massachusetts
- Michigan
- Minnesota
- Mississippi
- Missouri
- Montana

- Nebraska
- Nevada
- New Hampshire
- New Jersey
- New Mexico
- New York
- North Carolina
- North Dakota
- Ohio
- Oklahoma
- Oregon
- Pennsylvania
- Rhode Island

- South Carolina
- South Dakota
- Tennessee
- Texas
- Utah
- Vermont
- Virginia
- Washington
- Washington D.C.
- West Virginia
- Wisconsin
- Wyoming

- Puerto Rico Statehood

lect sites for individual teachers or schools, they find many sites that can be placed directly into the Homework Center. For example, youth librarians in Multnomah County were puzzled several years ago when students began asking them for materials on "biomes." *What* were biomes? Librarians rapidly learned that biomes were specific types of environments, such as the high desert or the tropical rainforest. They also rapidly discovered that in 1996 and 1997 there were more good Web sites on biomes (at least sites that called them biomes, which is important when you're working with students looking specifically for that word) than there were books. So there is now an impressive collection of biome Web sites in the Homework Center. In 1996 many of the youth librarians in individual branches of Multnomah County Library were bookmarking the biome sites on their reference desk Web stations for their own use. Now, due to Kate's campaign to make sure every librarian in the system knows about and uses the Homework Center, those same youth librarians are likely to e-mail her with the URL and title of a really good site that helps with a current assignment.

The Homework Center adds value in several ways. The sites are all annotated, so that students, parents, and teachers will have some idea of what is included in a site before they go there. The URL of each site is on the page to examine, so the page can be printed out in a library and taken elsewhere to look at the sites another time. Having the URL on the page also allows students to test their skills at analyzing what kind of site—government, corporate, college, or individual—it is before visiting it. (See the section on evaluating URLs in chapter 3.)

National Cathedral School (Washington, D.C.)
Upper School Library Internet Database
http://www.ncs.cathedral.org/library/upper/ncsid/

The National Cathedral School (NCS) for Girls is a private school in Washington, D.C. Katey Craver, Mary Misch, and Sue Gail Spring, the Upper School Library staff, debuted their Upper School Library Web site at the beginning of the 1996–1997 school year. After its debut, the three spent six months developing and coding the NCS Internet Database, a collection of hundreds of Web sites that meet the particular needs of both the Upper and Lower Schools. The three upper school librarians reviewed, categorized, and keyworded more than 1,700 sites and input the data using Microsoft Access.

Unfortunately, the sites are not annotated. (See figure 4.4.) However, the selection of sites and the obvious care that went into their selection makes the Internet Database a site for other libraries to study. The Homework Help page, for example, features a collection of "Ask a . . ." sites,

Figure 4.4   National Cathedral School's Internet Database Index Page

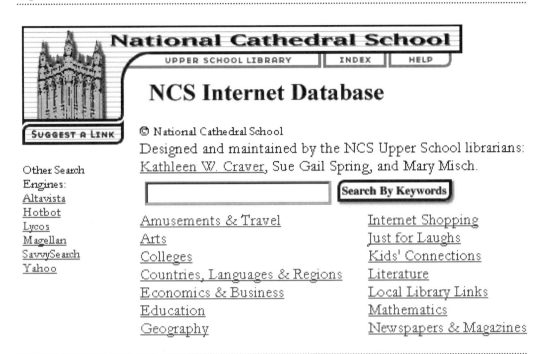

such as Ask a Science Expert, Ask a Volcanologist, and even "Ask the Amish." (Well, you don't really ask the Amish, who don't use PCs; you ask an "Amish expert" at the Mennonite Information Center in Lancaster County, Pennsylvania.) Craver admits that maintaining the Internet Database, with the help of the URL Minder application, is rough but worth it; it "requires our attention several hours each week."

The Database has proven its value to Craver. She is pleased that the Database "has enabled excellent Internet sites to be seamlessly integrated into our curriculum." Library staff use the Database to teach search strategies during the seventh grade's week-long library skills unit. Faculty members direct students to relevant Internet sites by asking the library staff to add the site to the Database with the teacher's name as a keyword, thus allowing students to quickly access specific sites for specific assignments.

Kathy Schrock's Guide for Educators
http://www.capecod.net/schrockguide/

Kathy Schrock's guide is not a library site but a site for teachers. It's worth mentioning, however, because it is one of the oldest education-oriented Web directories, founded in June 1995. It now contains more than 1,400

Figure 4.5   Kathy Schrock's Guide for Educators Page

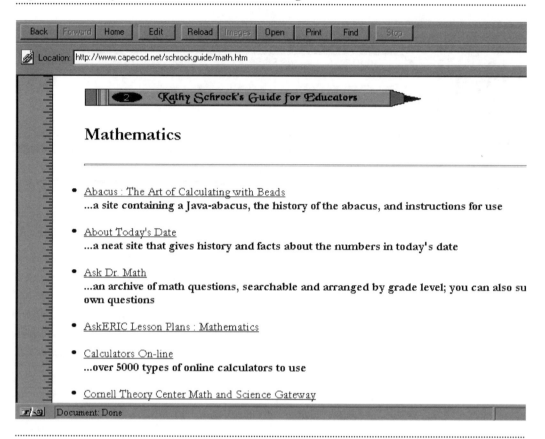

sites. (See figure 4.5.) It also includes a set of Net-oriented training courses and materials, such as a slide show on search strategies and a Web-site evaluation called "How to Find It and What to Do With It When You Do." Schrock encourages teachers and school librarians to create "content-rich home pages" for their schools that will boost the amount of useful K–12 content on the Web. Her site also contains a copy of the Fry Readability Graph, in case educators wish to check out the grade-level readability of an Internet site.

How to Build a YPWRC

One fact about creating a *good* (note the italics) Web site of any kind is undeniable: it's a lot of work. Finding sites, evaluating them, and assigning them subject headings take time. Checking links, locating sites with "temporary value" (such as the site for whatever Olympics is about to come up), changing URLs and annotations, and other maintenance tasks are time-consuming tasks. Who is going to do all this work?

For most successful YPWRCs, their librarian-creators understand the value of the Web as a reference tool; they have spent a lot of time looking at thousands of sites. They have spent a lot more time searching for pages to answer reference questions with mixed success and have decided to do something about it themselves. They learn how to code in HTML (hypertext markup language); think at length about how students look for information; and plan out a page, then several pages, and then a true collection of Web sites.

If you're beginning a YPWRC now and would like some advice, here's ours. The first rule of building an effective Web site, like the first rule in accomplishing any project, is plan first, build second. Expect your Web site to grow—perhaps much larger than you ever thought it would—and plan accordingly. Most librarians are neither inclined nor prepared to do all this work, so we want to warn you that, as in doing anything well, you must begin by really caring about assembling your page or pages and by really wanting to assemble them. The following sections, broken first into preparation and then into construction phases, outline how to build a YPWRC.

Preparation

Here are our recommendations for preparing to create your own YPWRC. They will give you a good foundation for creating a Web site design.

Learn HTML, or at least gain some idea how it works. Several good HTML editor programs are on the market, such as Adobe PageMill and Microsoft Front Page, and they will let you design and build Web pages quickly and easily. However, HTML editors can't do everything, and if you don't understand how HTML works, you may find editor programs formatting your pages just as you *don't* want them. Learn how to code at least the basics by hand (in particular, how to format text and create hyperlinks). Many books on the subject and many more sites on the Web itself can introduce you to the basics if you're a "self-taught" kind of person. If you're not, plenty of community colleges and other local institutions teach basic HTML.

Target your YPWRC. For whom will your YPWRC be intended? For ages birth through age 18? Fourth through eighth graders? Sixth graders through high schoolers? Kids and parents? If you are intending to create pages for distinct groups, separate the groups and label them clearly. If a site will be valuable for both middle schoolers and teachers, put it in both lists.

Make a list of the topics you will need to cover. If you know that every November there will be a big fifth-grade assignment about various Native American nations and their costumes, food, and art, you will want to put those things on your list. Ask other librarians and local teachers to help you come up with a list of all the typical homework questions that are likely to be asked in your locality over the course of a typical year.

Study other YPWRCs and similar Web directories for an adult or a general audience. What topics are sites broken into? How many sites are listed for a typical topic? How are the sites formatted on the page? How easy is it to navigate between topics and subtopics in the directory? How many of the links are dead or have changed addresses? In a business plan, this step would be called "analyze the competition." Even though you aren't competing with these other sites, you should strive to do what they do better than they do it.

Borrow links from other sites you visit. If you go through all the homework help sites in the list in the webliography, visit each of their links, and choose the sites that will meet your needs, you can compile a list of basic sites for your directory in a short time. However, it is not considered professional behavior to grab an entire list of links from another site and add it to your page. Be selective and create your own list, adding favorite sites of your own. If you wish to use an entire collection of sites, link to that other collection or ask permission. You also should not borrow others' annotations without asking permission.

Thoroughly evaluate every Web site in your list. Simply because another library has selected a site for its list doesn't mean it's right for your users. Remember the Christmas site we mentioned at the beginning of this chapter with the X-rated version of "The Night Before Christmas"? You can avoid this kind of embarrassment by examining every Web site thoroughly before you add it to your YPWRC. You know what your young users are asking for. Do your selected sites include that information and enough of it? Is a specific bit of information on a specific page two or more clicks away from a site's home page easy or difficult to find? Does the advertising on a site overpower its content? For the moment, not enough sites on the wide variety of topics young people want and need to know about are professionally reviewed, so you will need to be reviewer *and* selector.

Collect URLs of sites of local and regional interest. Every year students have questions about the city, county, and state in which they live. If you live in California, for example, you know that students will be studying the Gold Rush and the California missions. Sites of local and regional interest aren't always in the "big" Web collections, and many of the local sites about cities are of the business-oriented variety and are aimed at adults with money to spend, not at students. You should be talking to local historical societies, newspapers, museums, and similar institutions and businesses to see whether they have sites on local topics that young people can use. If not, perhaps you can convince them to create some; perhaps your library or school can offer a local historical society or museum some server space and technical assistance in return for creating a local or regional history Web site. Some libraries have developed regional sites of their own. For example, look at the Tacoma (Washington) Public Library's Database of Washington Place Names Origins at http://www.tpl.lib.wa.us/nwr/placecgi.htm.

Construction

All pages in the directory should look and function in a similar way, and all pages should be clear. The National Cathedral School Internet Database has a beautifully clear and simple design with lots of content and lots of white space. Place your content into a centered 1 × 1 table with a width of perhaps 85 percent or 90 percent of the screen to give the page some margins.

Go easy on the graphics and colors. No, you don't need to stick with only black type on a white background, but you should use a minimum of graphics. Avoid loud colors, background art that makes the text difficult to read, and (please!) animated gifs. Use the fun stuff on your children's area home page and your directory of "fun and games" links—*not* in your YPWRC.

Your directory site should be easy to navigate. A rule to follow that goes back to the beginnings of Web design in 1994 is that everything on your site should be no more than three clicks from everything else. Have a clear table of contents, and don't nest pages more than three levels deeper than the table of contents. For example, if you want to break your animals list into separate pages, don't have a second table of contents appear on a separate page when your site visitor clicks on "animals" in your main table of contents. If you look at the Animals page in the Multnomah County Library Homework Center, you will see that the Animals sites are all on one long page. You can reach each section, say the Invertebrates section, of that long page easily by clicking on the list of sections at the top of the Animals page. No site link in the Homework Center is more than two clicks from the main table of contents; the same is true of the links in the National Cathedral School's Internet Database.

Place the sites and sections in each page into alphabetical order by title. Many of the Homework Help pages out there are jumbled in no particular order. This may sound nitpicky, but we have argued this point with other librarians who feel that, "Hey, it's the Web; people don't expect things to be in alphabetical order." Believe us, people using a library wonder what's going on if things aren't in alphabetical order. You may feel that kids don't care. Well, aren't we trying to set a good example of organizing information for students? It also shows pride in what you're doing.

When typing titles, use the title that's on the page, not the title you wish were on the page. Many sites out there have titles that are less than clear, particularly pages dealing with topics like the arts, literature, and poetry. All librarians know that there are certainly books with titles we wish we could change, too. For example, HarperCollins's Big Busy House at http://www.harperchildrens.com needs some explanation; it's a site of news and activities based on the publisher's books for children. If a site's title is less than clear, describe its content particularly well in an annotation.

Annotate every site. Few YPWRCs annotate their sites; this is both amazing and sad. When you're doing readers' advisory work with users, don't you (since you can't have read every book in the collection) and they like it better when you can hand them an annotated booklist? The role of the library in the age of the Web, once again, should be to add value to the resources out there by locating them, collecting them, organizing them, and *describing* them. There are at least ten astronomy sites out there, for example, suitable for kids. Why should a particular student or teacher use one of them over another? You should be telling them why.

Watch for those "slip through the cracks" sites. Most sites on the Web that are suitable for young people will fit pretty clearly into a standard group of topic headings. However, an occasional site that you want your clients to find will be hard to classify. Look, for example, at Professor Bubble's Official Bubble Homepage at http://bubbles.org/. It's a science site *and* a fun site; where should you list it? If you decide to put it under Science, where would you put it if your Science page is broken into the following subtopics:

astronomy, biology, chemistry, earth sciences, physics, science experiments, and weather? Dewey classifies "bubbles" as a topic under physics. Will young people find it there? You might want to list it on your Fun Sites page as well. Don't be hesitant to list a page in two locations.

Look particularly for sites that do what other media in your collection can't, and note their special capabilities in your annotations. When we do Web instruction in schools or for classes visiting the library, we often show them two sites. One is the Egyptian Hieroglyphics site at http://www2.torstar.com/rom/egypt. Here you can go to a hieroglyphics translator page where you can type anything you want, click a button, and have it translated into hieroglyphics in a matter of seconds. The other page we often show is the U.S. Census Bureau's Pop Clocks page at http://www.census.gov/ftp/pub/main/www/popclock.html. Here you can see the current estimated population of the United States and of the world. We ask students to memorize the last few numbers of the population, wait thirty seconds, and hit the Reload or Refresh button again. "Whoa!" many of the students say when they see how much the populations have grown in such a short time. No book or audiotape can do these things. However, remember (and stress to your young users) that the Web doesn't have everything, despite what is shown in the TV commercials. The Web is only *one* information source, alongside books and other media.

Check your spelling and grammar before putting your pages online. Nothing is more embarrassing than a site from a public or school library that contains misspellings, misplaced apostrophes, and grammar errors. For better or worse, the public expects the work of librarians to be grammatically perfect. Be sure to have someone who is not involved in the site—and has an editor's eye— read over the text of your pages.

Check your pages, once they're online, on a variety of computers, monitors, and browsers. Remember that everyone's equipment is not the same as yours.

If you have a 17″ monitor, remember that many computer users have 15″ monitors, and vice versa. The monitor size definitely will affect the appearance of your pages, as will the screen settings on your monitor (for example, 640 × 480 versus 800 × 600 resolution).

If you're a Windows PC user, how does your site look on a Mac (and vice versa)?

How does the site look under older versions of America Online's browser, which many AOL subscribers are still using?

If you're using Internet Explorer 4.01 (the current version at this writing), how does the page look in Netscape Navigator 3.04? If you upgrade your browser whenever a new version comes out, remember that most people don't. Remember that there are still folks out there using the text-only browser Lynx or turn off the image loading to speed things up.

Do all of your graphics include "ALTs" (text tags that describe graphics), so text-only users will be able to understand and use your page?

Don't use frames, sound, or animation for directories of links. Young people who have grown up with electronic media are often easily distracted by anything that flashes, makes noise, or moves. Frames are not good for library sites because our goal is to reach as many users as we can, and frames make it harder to find the URLs of linked sites, to see an entire linked page, and to print without confusion. Keep your pages as simple and clear as possible. You don't want users to *stay* on your page; you want them to pass through your page to the materials they're seeking. You also don't want someone using an older browser to be unable to load your reference links because the page also contains a file their version of the browser can't handle.

Maintaining Your YPWRC

A YPWRC, whether it's a single page of what used to be bookmarks or a multipage directory of sites, cannot be put up on your server and ignored for months at a time. Have you ever gone to a What's New page on a site to see "news" items from six or eight months previously? If you put up a page with twenty-five links, probably two of those links will have died or changed within two or three months. You must consistently go through each of your links and make sure that your links haven't made that journey down Highway 404 (that is, they're dead and gone) or changed location.

So, plan to do some link-checking—or have someone check your links for you. If you have teenagers in your library who are interested in volunteering, link checking is an excellent volunteer job, particularly if you are willing to take some time to train the teenagers in what to look for. When you or your volunteers check links, you need to know if a site has moved, changed its name, or changed its management. Small Web sites sometimes are bought by large companies, sites merge, and sites break into separate components. Note any or all of these changes on a paper or electronic form, and change URLs and annotations accordingly.

How much time this link-checking task involves will depend on the size of your directory. If you have a single page with a few dozen links, you can check them all in fifteen or twenty minutes once a month. If your site is more ambitious, with many pages and hundreds of links, plan to check links for three to four hours every other week or so.

In the webliography you'll see a list of link-checking tools. Try several of them on your site and make a bookmark on your PC to the one you like best. Several of them have the capability to check all the links on your page in the space of a few minutes. However, these link checkers cannot verify the content of a site. Perhaps the content has changed or the site merely features a "we have moved" sign and its new URL. If you don't catch that message, the next thing you know the site will have disappeared.

Finding New Sites for Your YPWRC

An important part of the maintenance process is adding new links. The following list includes suggestions about ways to learn of great new pages out there of interest to you.

> *Check out the "what's new, what's cool, what's useful" kinds of Web sites and print articles.* These appear everywhere (again, see the webliography for some sites we like). Your local newspaper may run such a column, or it may spotlight local people who have created worthwhile Web sites. Magazines such as *Yahoo Internet Life* are constantly reviewing and spotlighting new sites. (Always take computer magazine and newspaper reviews with a large chunk of salt—these kinds of reviewers are typically more concerned with a site's "coolness quotient" than its utility in a school or library situation.) *On-Line, Off-Line* (http://www.rockhillpress.com/onoff/onoffint.htm) is a subscription-based magazine that gathers all types of materials under one theme in each issue. It always includes suggested Web sites.

> *Some libraries, library publications, and public/school/cooperative library systems produce What's New pages.* El Dorado County Library in Placerville, California, for example, publishes a What's Hot on the Internet This Week page at http://www.el-dorado.ca.us/~lib-pl/thisweek.htm. *Library Journal* (http://www.ljdigital.com/) and *School Library Journal* (http://www.slj.com/) and their Web sites also spotlight sites with an emphasis on topics and approaches that are useful to librarians and library users.

Put up a form on your library site asking for suggestions. Take a look at the form developed by the authors for the ALSC Notable Children's Websites Committee shown in figure 4.6. You're welcome to go to the form, at http://www.ala.org/alsc/nwsccrit.html#nwscsug and borrow the code between the <FORM> and </FORM> tags on this page. You must talk with your automation department or Internet service provider, however, to code the <FORM ACTION> tag that accesses your server's CGI (Common Gateway Interface) script correctly. (Ask your automation person if you don't know what we're talking about—he or she will know what we mean.) Adding such a form can be dangerous, however, if you fear an overloaded e-mail box. You may have a few submissions (a few of *those* unprintable) from young users of your site. However, in our experience, 90 percent of submissions will come from small

Figure 4.6 Site Suggestion Form

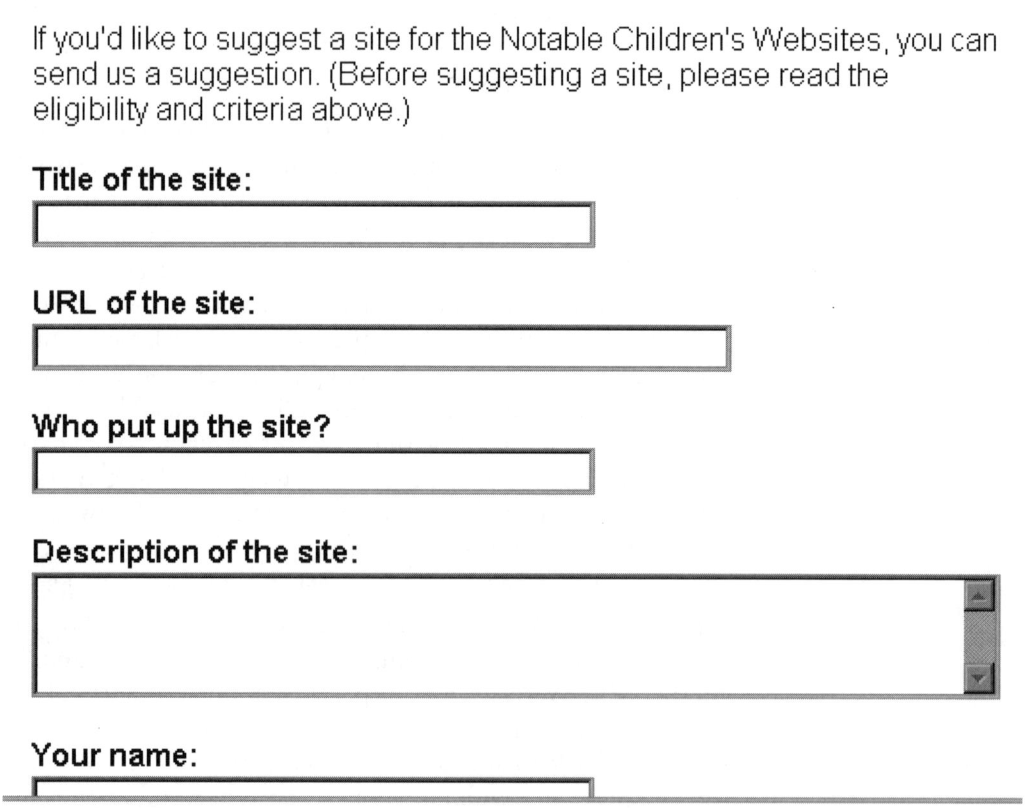

If you'd like to suggest a site for the Notable Children's Websites, you can send us a suggestion. (Before suggesting a site, please read the eligibility and criteria above.)

Title of the site:

URL of the site:

Who put up the site?

Description of the site:

Your name:

Web-based businesses and service organizations in your area in search of some free publicity. If you're willing to look at all the sites that sound promising, the occasional diamond will poke through from the rough.

If you've promoted your YPWRC, colleagues will send you sites. Once your staff knows how useful your site is, they'll send you sites they see on TV, read about in the newspaper, or find while helping students over the desk.

The best way is to talk with anyone and everyone in your area who works with both young people and the Web. Our favorites are local school "Web-activists" such as teachers who use the Web in their classrooms and local school district technology specialists. They should have favorite sites they'll be happy to share with you, and remember to talk with them every six months or so to ask for new ideas and URLs.

Go through your site and do topic searching on the Net for what's missing. You and your fellow YPWRC committee members should promise each other to go through every section in your site at least every three months and add something new.

Publicizing Your YPWRC

Here is a sad fact, however, about YPWRCs—most kids will not use them on their own without encouragement. If you leave them alone with a Web station, they'll go instantly to Navigator's Net Search button or to Yahoo or HotBot to find things and ignore your hard-built YPWRC. They'll ignore it, that is, unless you put its URL in their faces at every opportunity. You must train them to think that your YPWRC is a good place to look.

So now comes the final task: making sure that everyone in your community hears about your YPWRC—particularly those who can give your YPWRC a boost. If you're a public librarian, tell your local school districts' technology specialists, teachers, and media specialists that it's there. If you're a school library media specialist, tell your public children's librarian about it as well as all the teachers in your building, all the parents you happen to chat with, and media specialists in other districts or buildings. Don't do it once; do it over and over.

Make sure your YPWRC has a link on your institution's home page. Does your library or school have a newsletter? Make sure the URL of your YPWRC is printed in it—not only in one issue, but in every issue, forever, for as long as your YPWRC is online. Print or photocopy some bookmarks with the URL featured prominently, leave them on the reference and circulation desks and beside your Web stations, and replenish the stack when all the bookmarks are gone.

Don't just leave the URL for your YPWRC around in print. Demonstrate the Web-reference collection for everyone you can, all the time, every chance you get. Make it part of every Internet class, and make curriculum-related sites from your YPWRC a part of every faculty in-service. Go to staff meetings and talk about it and show it off if you can. Show it to individual teachers, parents, and students and to groups of teachers, parents, and students. The more people see it and know about it, the more likely they are to bookmark it, the more it will be used, and the more people will tell you about the great site they just found.

A Final Suggestion

It is your commitment and that of your colleagues during these first few years of the Web in education that will set the stage for everything that will come after. The companies that will one day design the commercial Internet directory services many of us will be using are looking at what we're doing with the Web now. The sites we design and create now will influence the role of libraries in making the Web more comprehensible for the general public into the next few decades. Librarians serving young people should be taking an active part in constructing that role.

It's easy to feel, um, tangled in the Web sometimes. That's why we make a final suggestion in this chapter. We ask all of you to archive a copy of your first (or current, if you have one up already) Homework Help page on a floppy disk, storage medium (such as a Zip disk), or your hard drive, exactly as it first goes up on your server. Let a year or more pass. Then go back and open that file or set of files again in your browser.

If you began by following our suggestions, or by using a process similar to our suggestions, you will be amazed at how much the current version of your page outshines the original. During that year you will have learned some new tricks and ideas about how to design access to information. You will have continued to look at and learn from other libraries' and schools' Web sites and YPWRCs. You will have attended local, regional, and national workshops and classes from library associations, education organizations, and universities. You will have experimented with various new ideas on your YPWRC, and it will have changed for the better.

Then let another year or so pass, and if the current version of your browser (or whatever you call information-site-access software then) allows you to do it, look at your YPWRC again. You'll be amazed at what you've accomplished in two years.

Notes

1. Stephen Toub, "Adding Value to Internet Connections," *Library Hi Tech* 15, no. 3–4 (1997): 149.

2. Toub, 149.

5

The Web in the Real-World Library

This chapter is about all those "little things" that are going to come up if you have Web terminals, particularly public-access Web terminals, in your library. All of them have some effect on the quality of reference services you can provide to young people, and all are things people will ask you about more than once.

Text, Graphics, Fonts, and Printing

Because it isn't possible to "check out" a Web site and take it home, and because many students need records of the sites they visit, you are not serving your users well without some way to print out Web pages. Color ink jet printers, which are now reasonably priced and reliable, are the best printers to attach to Net terminals in a typical library situation. Some libraries charge ten to twenty-five cents a page for color ink jet printouts; others allow a certain number of free pages, such as the first three or five pages, and begin charging after that.

In chapter 2 we discussed finding images for students. During an average week of the school year you might help students locate color images on the Web of a Conestoga wagon, an orchid from the rainforest, the planet Saturn and each of its moons, a physical map of Saudi Arabia, and a menagerie of endangered animals. When you find such images, the students will often want to print them out or download them to a floppy disk.

Let's take a look at a typical printing situation. Suppose a student wants to print out part of the list of Newbery Medal winners and honor books from the ALSC Newbery Medal home page. This list is lengthy, and she only wants to print out the winners and honor books from the years 1922 to 1940. Once the page is on the screen using Navigator, she can select Print Preview from the File menu to page through the document and select only those pages with the winners and honor books from those years. Using the magnifying glass tool in the lower left corner of each page, she can also see how many pages it would take to print out the entire document (eighteen pages on our test PC). A great many Web pages are extremely long, and when a library charges by the page for printing—or when the student simply doesn't want to kill too many trees—Print Preview is a handy tool.

Internet Explorer handles printing slightly differently. Under Print a choice of Print Selection is offered. If you highlight the text or the part of a Web page you want to print, you can print only that particular section.

Printing Text

Remember also that the font and the font size in which your text appears on the screen make a difference when you print. So do the background and text colors. These facts aren't as obvious as you might think because not everyone knows the following:

1. Text size (or type or font size) is measured in points. On many computer screens, one point equals one seventy-second of an inch. This depends of course on the resolution of your monitor; the higher the total number of pixels on your screen (1024 × 768, say, versus 800 × 600), the smaller type will appear on your screen. Twelve points is the default size used by most Web browsers for screen text, but the standard sans serif fonts—Arial and Helvetica—appear to take up more space than Times Roman, the standard serif font. (See figure 5.1.) If text appears in twelve-point Arial on the page and you have pages and pages of text to

Figure 5.1   Apparent Differences in Type Sizes of Two Fonts

| Here is a test comparing the sizes of two different fonts. This font is Times New Roman. Do you see how it "looks" smaller than Arial, even though it's officially the same size? | Here is a test comparing the sizes of two different fonts. This font is Arial. Do you see how it "looks" larger than Times New Roman, even though it's officially the same size? |

print, you might save paper by temporarily switching the screen font (in the Preferences dialog boxes of your browser) to ten-point Times.

2. If you need really large type because of visual disabilities or the need to see the text from a distance, you can also set the type to a larger size, say twenty-four point Arial or Helvetica, before you print.

3. There's no doubt in the Web world that black pages and pages in other dark colors with white (or sometimes yellow) text are considered cool. Have you ever wanted to print a dark blue page with yellow type, and hit that Print button without thinking about it? We have, and it was embarrassing when, with a student watching, what looked at first like blank sheets of paper emerged from the printer. Only if you looked very closely could you see the illegible yellow type on the white paper. For most color printers, color backgrounds don't print (and it's a good thing; imagine how quickly you'd run out of ink cartridges in a typical library if they did), but color text does. You can set the Preferences of your browser temporarily to switch to black text. This isn't always the case in all browser/printer combinations, however, especially with black-and-white printers; you should run a print test of pages with dark backgrounds in your network environment.

4. Some libraries allow members of the public to change settings; others have them locked up from public alteration. If the latter is the case for you, the Web stations at the reference desk should be modifiable so that you may print out documents for your users. Please, however, if you allow browser changes and show students how to change settings temporarily, ask them to be considerate of other users and change them back when they are through. Users should see Web pages with the colors, graphics, and backgrounds the designer intended.

Printing Pictures

Another typical situation is that a student will want a photo or graphic to use in a paper. We'll deal with the copyright issues of "borrowing" text and illustrations from online sources later in this chapter, but students are coming to rely on the Web as a source of graphics for both school and fun. If your printers are all black and white, it is best—if the student has a choice of pictures—to choose a high-contrast graphic with light lights and dark darks, so it will translate well to laser or black-and-white ink jet printing.

If a color printer isn't available in the library and a student has access to a color printer at home or elsewhere—or wants to use a digital copy of the graphic in, say, a ClarisWorks presentation for school—it is better to download the image from the Web to a floppy disk. Many libraries, however, have policies prohibiting insertion of "strange" floppies into library PCs. Since your users can introduce viruses to your system this way, this prohibition is not an unwise policy up to a point. We have heard stories of (and seen personally) hackers secreting floppies in their jackets and backpacks and inserting them to deliberately crash systems in schools and libraries when (they thought) the staff weren't looking.

With so much useful material available on the Net, however, it is a shame to prohibit students from saving copies of graphics, text, sound files, and other media on disk. Some libraries give away or sell blank floppy disks for this very reason, often using disks in bright colors so they can easily spot anyone with a generic black floppy. Some of these libraries will confiscate nonlibrary floppies if they have reason to suspect that a user is either copying software from the library PC or "up to some funny business."

For those libraries that do allow users to insert the library's or the user's floppies, most users (but not all) know how to save a copy of any graphic on the Web. That is, they place the cursor arrow or hand (this will work on graphics that are links, too) over the desired graphic and press and release the right mouse button on a Windows machine. On a Mac, they hold down the mouse button. In both cases, a menu will appear that allows them to save the graphic to disk. Because the majority of images on the Web are 80K or less in file size, users can save fifteen or more images to a blank floppy.

Two basic graphics formats are used on the Web: the GIF format (CompuServe Graphics Interchange Format) and the JPG or JPEG format (for Joint Photographic Experts Group, the group that settled on the format standard). The GIF format is typically used for line art and graphics with a limited number of colors, such as the navigation buttons and bars seen on many Web sites, logos, and other artwork. Graphics you see on the Web that are animated (the little e-mail box that keeps opening and closing until you want to slam it shut, for example) or that are irregularly shaped with "transparent" areas through which you can see colored backgrounds are always GIFs.

If you create Web pages for your library, knowledge of graphics formats is essential. The JPEG (or .jpg) format is typically used for photographs. Photos usually contain a wider range of colors and shades, which make for larger file sizes, than graphic art. In figure 5.2, the photo is a JPEG file and the words and book image are GIF files. JPEG documents are severely compressed to keep file sizes as small as possible. If you have ever worked with a graphics program like Paint Shop Pro, Color It!, or Photoshop, you will see how a scanned photograph can be reduced from 350K to 35K by converting it from TIFF (Tagged Image File Format, a

Figure 5.2   JPEG and GIF Images

standard format for scanner documents), or BMP (bitmap), or PSD (Photo-shop) formats (which Web browsers do not handle) to JPEG. JPEGs are always square or rectangular.

Fashionable Web design often consists of a great many images and bits of text jumbled together on the screen. What if a young user would like to be able to print a single image on an otherwise blank piece of paper? You can open the image alone by holding down the right mouse button on a Windows PC or by holding down the mouse button on a Mac to choose View Image—and you'll be taken to the location of that image. It will appear alone in the upper-left corner of the screen (unfor-tunately, there's no way to change that), and then you can print it.

Sites that use frames can be real pains when it comes to helping stu-dents find and print pictures. A good rule when you're doing reference work is that if a site offers a choice between a frames version and a non-frames version, choose the latter. Frames can be very useful if you are progressing through a great many pages in a site and need to continually return to a navigation bar to move to new pages. However, too often frames sites seem to have been designed as more of a show-off for the site's creator than as a useful presentation.

The content portion of a frames site typically appears in the largest of the frames, and each of the content pages that appears in this frame has a separate URL. It is the URL of the outer frame page, usually the table-of-contents portion, that appears in the location box. Thus you often don't know the URL of a particular content page in a frames site, and if you try to print that content page, you might be able to print only the material in the outer frame. You will be most successful printing the "inner" content parts of frames sites if you click within the segment of the page you wish to print before pressing that Print button.

"Plug-In" Files and Multimedia

When some Web sites appear on your screen, you might see a big white box containing a small puzzle-piece icon that doesn't make any sense. You might also see a dialog box that tells you that your browser lacks a particular "plug-in" file. These files are pieces of software that must be placed in the same directory as your browser to play certain kinds of multimedia files. Examples are RealAudio files, QuickTime video files, and Shockwave files.

Downloading and installing any of the various plug-in player files can be tedious. When you download the Shockwave animation file player, for example, you must go to the Macromedia site or one of its "mirror sites." (Macromedia is the company that manufactures Flash, the application used to create Shockwave files.) Then you click through several other buttons in a process reminiscent of a corporate voice mail system until you can download the file. Once the file downloads, you must close your browser, run the Setup file, and install the player into your browser's directory. Then you must restart your browser and return to the page with the Shockwave animation. Some of these animations make all this tedium worth it, however; check out the pie-throw game on the Cyber-Jacques site http://www.cyberjacques.com/ or, if you have a *flexible* sense of humor, the Celebrity Slugfest http://www.celebrityslugfest.com/.

So far we have dealt with text and graphics, but other kinds of files are available on the Web, particularly sound, video, and game files, that are quite attractive to young people. Several multimedia companies have created software to produce these files, which means there are several competing formats for sound, video, and animation.

Sound Format Plug-Ins

Examples of sound file formats are AIFF files, MOD files, WAV files, and RealAudio or RAM files. RealAudio files will let you listen to audio as it downloads, but they require a RealAudio player, which must be downloaded and installed in your system if you are using some older Web browsers. There are also specialized electronic musical instrument files (MIDI files). Most of these will play on an average PC with a sound card. Many libraries, however, do not have Web station PCs with sound cards; therefore the sound will not play and users will need to close a dialog box to that effect.

WAV files are perhaps the most common format for Windows 95 or Windows NT sound files. When they download from a server, a small sound-file window will appear onscreen. (See figure 5.3.). The window will remain blank until the sound is completely downloaded; then "play" and "stop" buttons and a volume control will appear in the little window. By clicking the right mouse button, you can save a WAV file (and some other downloadable media files, too) to your A: or C: drive.

Figure 5.3   WAV Sound File Window

Video and Animation Plug-Ins

Dealing with video and animation files is a little trickier. One common video format is the QuickTime (MOV) file; another type is the MPEG file (which is also an audio format). QuickTime is a common format used for video files on CD-ROM disks, and when you install a multimedia CD-ROM on your system, it will frequently require you to install a QuickTime player. VIVO is a proprietary video file format optimized for 28.8 modem downloads, and it requires a VIVO player, which must be downloaded and installed. If you see the puzzle piece icon (see figure 5.4), it means you're missing the correct plug-in file. Figure 5.5 shows a prompt to get the plug-in.

Figure 5.4   Netscape's Mysterious Puzzle
Piece Icon

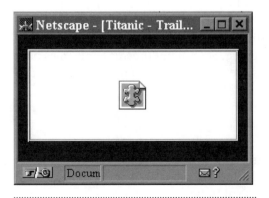

Figure 5.5   Netscape's Prompt
for a Plug-In

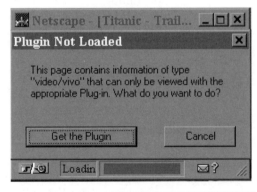

Other Plug-Ins

In a library environment, you will also need to have Adobe Acrobat Reader installed on all your Web stations (especially in a public library around tax time). This is an application that can deliver printable paper documents to your browser formatted exactly as in the original. Acrobat is frequently used for print publications, such as academic journal articles with graphs and diagrams, that are published on the Web.

Although newer versions of Navigator and Internet Explorer include many plug-in files, there seem to be new formats—and new versions of the older plug-ins—appearing regularly. The best rule for handling multimedia formats on library Web stations is to ask users to come to you when these "plug-in file missing" dialog boxes appear. You (or your automation services manager) should be the one to decide what is to be downloaded and installed on your system. This also means that you should be talking constantly with your most technologically adept students or colleagues, asking them what audio, video, and animation formats your Web stations should be prepared to play.

Copyright Issues

One of the thorniest issues in the world of the Internet in general is that of intellectual property and copyright. Any librarian who has, over the past ten years, worried about whether it was legal to show a videotape rented from the video store for home viewing to an after-school group or to read a picture book over the local cable TV station is familiar with how sticky these areas can get. Over the Internet, unfortunately, the complexities just grow worse because so much material is available online at no charge and because it's so easy to "borrow" what's there.

Many teachers and librarians believe that because what they do is noble and virtuous, and because they're not doing the wonderful things they do educating our children for profit, whatever they do with copyrighted materials with young people is "fair use." They believe also that if they use copyrighted material but cite the creator, using the copyrighted material is all right. Both beliefs are wrong.

An excellent page is available on the Benton Foundation's Web site that discusses how intellectual-property issues affect the use of the Net in education. (See the webliography.) Following are a few issues that may come up while doing reference work in the library that deal with fair use of copyrighted materials. (*Note:* Copyright law is a messy area, and we aren't lawyers. So we're not claiming that what we say here is the absolute truth. Check the U.S. Copyright Office site for more information on copyright and fair use under U.S. law, and, of course, be aware that copyright laws differ from country to country.)

Almost everything on the Internet is protected by copyright, from online games to personal e-mail messages. This is true whether that little c-in-a-circle is there or not. Two types of material on the Internet are considered to be in the public domain and free to copy. These are most works published more than 75 years ago and works published by the U.S. government. The nineteenth- and early twentieth-century works put online by Project Gutenberg are good examples of the former. The many sites maintained by the many entities of the U.S. government (the ".gov" sites) are the latter. These two general guidelines are not ironclad, however. For example, you may find some Chinese poetry written in the year 1084 on the Net. Can you copy it without permission? Probably not, unless it's in the original Chinese. Translations of works from other languages are almost always copyrighted. Before copying anything from the Net that you think might be in the public domain, you should check carefully for copyright notices.

If what you want to copy falls outside these two areas (and more than 90 percent of what's on the Web does), are you able to copy it? Maybe. It depends on what you're copying and how you plan to use it. If a student is copying material from a site to use as part of a homework assignment, it may seem like fair use, and it probably would be considered so in a court. However, there are no absolutes under fair use; the law is slippery.

When we train students in Web site evaluation, we include a brief introduction to intellectual property, although we don't call it that. We call it "quoting, copying, or stealing?" On its Web site, the Bellingham (Washington) School District has posted a copyright compliance policy on the use of copyrighted materials in education. Here (quoted with permission) is a portion of that policy. The entire Bellingham School District Copyright Policy is worth reading if you are interested in fair use and intellectual property, both online and off.

Under the "fair use" doctrine, unauthorized reproduction of copyrighted materials is permissible for such purposes as criticism, comment, news reporting, teaching, scholarship or research. If duplicating or changing a product is to fall within the bounds of fair use, these four standards must be met for any of the foregoing purposes:

A. *The purpose and character of the use.* The use must be for such purposes as teaching or scholarship and must be nonprofit.

B. *The nature of the copyrighted work.* Staff may make single copies of the following for use in research, instruction, or preparation for teaching: book chapters; articles from periodicals or newspapers; short

stories, essays, or poems; and charts, graphs, diagrams, drawings, cartoons, or pictures from books, periodicals, or newspapers in accor-
dance with these guidelines.

C. *The amount and substantiality of the portion used.* In most cir-
cumstances, copying the whole of a work cannot be considered fair
use; copying a small portion may be if these guidelines are followed.

D. *The effect of the use upon the potential market for or value of the
copyrighted work.* If resulting economic loss to the copyright holder can
be shown, even making a single copy of certain materials may be an infringement, and making multiple copies presents the danger of greater
penalties.[1]

To Copy or Not to Copy?

In almost all cases, copying material for an individual's homework assignment is considered fair use when only the student and teacher are
involved. Things get much trickier, however, when a student or teacher
(or librarian) is creating a Web page and using materials from other Web
sites or scanning in copyrighted materials from books and other printed
materials for posting on a site that is accessible to the world.

Let's go farther. It's common for young people to print photos or artwork of things they consider cool from the Web. If a young person using
a Web station in the library is printing off multiple copies of pictures of
TV show characters to put up in his locker at school and to give to his
friends for their lockers, is this "fair use"? Almost definitely not, although
it's doubtful that anyone will "come after" the student. The Web is filled
with sites of copyrighted performances put up by fans of bands, movies,
cartoons, and TV shows, most of them scanned from magazines and
recorded from albums without permission. Young people (and a few not
so young) will then save sound files to their hard drives and print out
pictures to hang on lockers and refrigerators. This kind of permission-
less copying and printing happens all the time on library PCs, but that
doesn't make it legal. The role of libraries in providing PCs—which are,
whether we like it or not, a means of copying copyrighted material—is
becoming similar to its role in providing copy machines.

The public nature of Web pages changes things, too. Many of the
students and teachers you serve—and you too—may have personal or
work-related Web sites. There is a big difference between printing pictures for your personal use and putting up copies of those pictures on
your own site, whether for an educational purpose or not. If, let's say,
you "borrow" some photographs from nature photographers' Web sites
and post them on your personal home page, it isn't sufficient to credit
the photographers, or even to credit them and put up a link to their sites.

This is true even if you aren't selling anything but are putting up their pictures only because you like them so much you want everyone to see them. You must ask the photographers' permission to copy their photographs, especially if you will be posting them elsewhere on the Web where they will be available to the general public. In situations like this one, it's better to link to the photographers' sites (which is, by the way, legal to do without asking). But if you put their pictures on your Web site, you are stealing their sites' uniqueness.

If students and teachers ask questions about whether to ask for permission, it is a good general rule to ask for permission if you aren't sure. If the site from which you wish to use material has an e-mail link to its maintainer, it's possible to e-mail a site's creator and receive permission within a few days to use material from the site. Sometimes in granting you permission, a creator (writer, artist, photographer, etc.) will specify exactly what words to use in the credit line on your site; if not, ask. It's a good idea to include near the borrowed material something like "©1998 Matilda Brown; used with permission." You can usually find out the correct copyright credit from the creator when you ask for permission.

Many people are willing to let you put their pictures on a site for educational, nonprofit purposes if you give them credit and (sometimes) a link to their sites. Asking permission, however, is most successful with text and graphics that are not part of a "big money" site. Don't expect Warner Brothers or Sony to grant permission to put photos of movie or cartoon characters from their sites on a student's personal home page. There are plenty of sites on the Web offering free or public domain graphics that can be copied with no problem, but check the site and look for the clearly stated right to do so.

This issue is a critical and constantly changing one, and it is too complex to cover properly here. Refer to the sites listed in the webliography under "Legal Issues, Policies, and Safety" for more complete, up-to-date information.

Setting Up and Managing Your Net Terminals

How are your Net terminals set up? In an ideal library (all right; go ahead, laugh), you should have one reference terminal, not accessible to users, for each reference librarian on duty during the busiest times. These should be networked to a color ink jet printer. There should be as many public-access Net terminals as your institution can afford, and these should be networked as well, two or three to a color ink jet printer. Typically, Net terminals are stuck out on the floor wherever it's convenient. This is true particularly when a building is older and crowded and where out-lets are few and connections hard to add. If you are lucky, the most convenient spot will be near the reference desk (that is, the place from which a librarian typically answers questions, even if it doubles as a circulation desk).

If the Net terminals are far from the reference desk, expect problems for users and reference staff. Users will get lost on the Web, search engines will let them down, the browser will crash, they will be greeted with a message that tells them they lack a particular plug-in file, and they'll type ".com" when they should have typed ".gov."

Don't worry, your users need your help, even if they don't speak that need aloud. Many young people see the Net as "their" thing, a cool thing that has nothing to do with the librarians, and they think they can do everything themselves. If you watch users sitting at the screen you will often see them staring, clicking at things randomly, and looking lost. Surprise them. Step over to the Web stations periodically to say "Hi," and ask them if they're finding what they're looking for. Look them in the eyes rather than looking at their screens. If you do that regularly, and get to know the young people who use the Web stations most, you will find yourself hearing questions more frequently. If you've established with your young users that you do know how to navigate the Net, on a typical day you may be called over to the table of Net terminals many times. It may be only to explain what a DNS entry is and why the video-game-tips site the user wants to find doesn't seem to be there.

Net Station "Abuse"

Keeping the terminals far from the reference desk is also an invitation for what is, um, politely called "abuse." We're keeping this term in quotes because it means different things to different people. For purposes of this book, it means "using Web terminals in a way that causes problems for a particular library." Following are a few examples of what we feel most librarians would consider "abuse."

1. Eight teenagers congregate at the public library Net terminals and spend hours in chat rooms, reading text from the screen aloud and laughing. The words they read are often sexual in nature. An older male patron asks them to be quiet; one of the boys calls him a seven-letter name, and the older man threatens to punch the boy who insulted him.

2. Individual teenagers come to the public library after school and sit, sometimes until the library closes, at the terminals "chatting" or play-

ing MUDs (Multi-User Dungeon games). They sneak food and drinks in, despite library policy that says "No food or drink."

    3. Two thirteen-year-old boys come into the busy public library on a Saturday with the URL of an "adult" site on a scrap of paper. Whenever the staff isn't looking and a terminal is free, they pull up the site on the screen and walk away laughing loudly, leaving it there for the next user to find.

    4. In a high school computer lab, the teacher goes out of the room for a few minutes and a group of boys pull up an "adult" site and show it to some nearby girls, quickly exiting and restarting the browser when the teacher returns.

Are these problems Internet "abuse"? In a sense they are, because none of them would happen this way in a traditional, noncomputerized library. However, don't boys and girls still find books on human anatomy and laugh and giggle over the diagrams or leave the pages open to show their classmates? Don't young people pass "forbidden" magazines to each other behind grown-ups' backs? These are not "Internet problems" but behavior problems that can be and should be solved by writing and posting policies for Web station use that prohibit certain behaviors and then enforcing these policies fairly but clearly.

We, your authors, are choosing to sidestep the minefield of intellectual freedom, minors, libraries, and the Net because we believe that it's separate from behavior problems caused by the presence of Web stations in the library. Is filtering software appropriate for the public or school library environment, and if so, what kind? Are minors entitled to privacy while online, or should teachers or library staff be able to monitor their Net use? Issues such as these have been with us in the recent past, and they had nothing to do with the Net. Many librarians remember the controversies over whether to own, and to whom to circulate, Judy Blume's *Forever* and Michael Willhoite's *Daddy's Roommate*. In many communities the discussion goes on over whether those under 17 should be allowed to check out R-rated videos. With the Net now in our libraries, the ante, as they say, has been upped.

The Net is a scary place for many people because it's huge, sloppy, and uncontrolled. We think that its very nature makes it a wonderful metaphor for the world at large, and teachers and librarians who care can use it as a laboratory to help kids train for adult life. Students who learn, for example, how to evaluate a Web site—to look for the creator or sponsor of a site, how much the site tells you about itself, and the accuracy of its content—will gain skills they'll be able to use later buying a used car or dealing with a telephone solicitor. Nevertheless, certain portions of the media and some groups in our culture have been scaring us about the dangers on the Net for several years now, and those concerns will probably find their way into your library. There are plenty of places you can read about all sides of the issue. (See the webliography for a few suggestions.) Nevertheless, there are certain problems all libraries face when young people use Net terminals that have only a tangential relation to the issue of what content young people are accessing on our Web stations.

Unless your library is under the scrutiny of individuals and groups with social and political agendas, Net "abuse" problems can be kept under control without using filters or requiring parental signatures by setting definite policies and enforcing them. Different institutions have different requirements for use of Net terminals, and a full discussion of the topic would fill many more pages than we have.

Schools typically have a training system of some kind which students must pass to get what is often called an "Internet driver's license." Often computer lab teachers and media specialists will require that students attend a certain number of hours of classes in which they demonstrate they can responsibly handle cruising the Net. Public libraries sometimes require training programs, but usually do not, due to shortage of staff time. Most public library Net terminals are open for anyone to use. We also know how middle-school and high-school-aged young people like to "test" and see what they can get away with in all areas, not just with the Net.

Let's look again at the four Net abuse examples given earlier to see how the librarians involved dealt with them.

1. Dealing with the fight between the eight teenagers and the older patron was easy but unpleasant. While another staff member called 911, the supervisor on duty ordered all of them, including the older man, outside, and they left. However, solving this situation long term was not easy. This library had a sign-up sheet on a clipboard, and each user was supposed to limit himself or herself to one hour. Because there were eight teenagers in this group, each would sign up for an hour on different terminals, sometimes using false names, and "take over" the Net terminals for an entire afternoon or evening. Other library users wanted to use the Net terminals but were afraid to approach the group—as were some of the staff members—thus, the other users didn't get a chance.

The staff in this library met and devised a new policy. First, every user was allowed an hour a day at a Net terminal, period. The clipboard was moved to the reference desk, and each person who wanted to use the terminals had to sign up under the eyes of the staff and show a library card. The staff agreed to enforce the rules strictly, and they did. Although there was some grumbling from the eight teenagers, the problem stopped within a few weeks, as soon as each of the teenagers saw that everyone at the desk enforced the rules in exactly the same way for everyone. The teenagers came in less often, kept their voices down, and actually said "hello" to staff.

2. Once again, limiting the amount of time a single user could sign up for a terminal, and enforcing the limit fairly, alleviated much of the problem of monopolizing the terminals for long periods. There was an additional dimension to this problem: This situation occurred in a large library with terminals on multiple floors, and some of these users moved from floor to floor when their time was up. Because the staff did not feel it was worth the time having staff patrol all the floors looking for certain people, they are currently looking for software that will allow users on their network to enter their library card numbers and receive Net access for one or two hours per day.

The situation with food and drinks (which are bad for all library media, as we know) had developed because the staff felt they were too busy serving users to be library "police." The supervisor made it clear that all floor staff would offer to hold people's food and drinks behind the desk or ask them to finish consuming it outside. By enforcing this rule fairly, the worst of the problem vanished.

There is a great controversy among many library staff who manage Net terminals over whether chatrooms, MUDs, and e-mail are appropriate uses of a library Net terminal. In schools, unless such communication is under a teacher's or media specialist's supervision and is curriculum related, the answer is almost always "No." However, in a public library environment, appropriate usage is less clear cut. The libraries in this example did not have explicit "No chatroom, e-mail, or MUD use" policies, but it based its policies on the behavior of the terminal users, not the use they made of the terminals.

3. The example of the boys pulling up an "adult" site on screen is one of those situations that is particularly difficult for librarians who are defenders of an unfiltered Internet in a public library yet are sensitive to their patrons. "Adult" images in any context will offend a large number of library users, and we know that many adults expect the library to be a "safe" environment. (We know better, but that's another book.) The true problem developed in this situation when offended and angry library users began coming up to staff to complain about the "smut" on the terminal screens. The busy librarians apologized but weren't aware they had a "situation" until the third complaint. Soon a staff member caught the boys at work, took their names, and told them they were out of the library for the rest of the day, and their parents would be called if it happened again. That ended the situation. Once again, this was a behavior problem rather than an abuse of technology or an intellectual freedom issue.

4. The situation in the computer lab is tougher. In this school the boys were aware of the school's policy: They would lose all Internet

privileges for the rest of the year if caught breaking the rules, including looking at "inappropriate" sites on school computers. The teacher didn't even know this situation had occurred until one of the boys' parents (yes!) complained to the school. After talking with several class members, the boys who had brought up the site lost their Internet privileges. This was, clearly, another behavior problem.

Adolescents will be adolescents, and there is no way to completely ensure there will be no abuses among users of a library's Web stations. Abuses can be kept to a minimum if a library clearly sets down its policies to users and enforces those policies constantly, consistently, and fairly so that no users feel "singled out" for negative attention. Abuses can also be discouraged when a library offers training in the proper use of the Internet in general and that library's Web stations in particular. The next chapter considers some methods and ideas for training young people to make the best use of the Web and its resources.

Note

1. Bellingham (Wash.) School District, "Copyright Compliance Instruction," 23 Oct. 1996. Online. Available http://www.bham.wednet.edu/copyright.htm.

6

Training Young Users

As you can tell, we believe information literacy is important. It's important not only to find information on the Web *for* students but also important for them to learn *how* to find information on their own and to evaluate the information they find.

Local, Basic, and Flexible Training

When you train young people how to use the Web to find information (and you should be prepared to train them on the fly, even in a public library setting), think local, think basic, and be flexible.

When librarians get together in person or online, the same question is heard many times over: "When you get a question, should you use the opportunity to train the students to find the answer themselves, or should you just find the answer for them?" The answer, of course, is "It depends." Training young people to use the Web isn't much different from helping them learn to use the online catalog or a reference book with an index at the back of the book. Your ability to judge the need of the student and adjust the amount of "training" and your strategy for doing this should be considered part of reference work. It's a lot like the process of the "reference interview" when you answer any reference query.

Some young people are genuinely curious and want to know how to find things themselves. Others couldn't care less about where the answer comes from or how it arrives; they want only to get that answer and get out the door as quickly as they can. We can call these latter users "Wal-Mart students"; like Wal-Mart customers, they want to be led to the thing they're looking for, have it placed in their hands, and then be allowed to check out and leave. They don't want to be shown how the store is arranged or whether paper napkins are always found next to paper cups. For the reluctant "Wal-Mart student," it's usually not worth the trouble to show them how to find the answer in a public library, and in a school environment you may need to rely on a few tricks to coax their curiosity out.

On the other hand, how do you help curious students? Think *local*. Don't worry about what computer or browser students may have at home or anywhere else. Show them how to find the answer with the collection and on the equipment in front of you. Have some local Web pages—pages you or your colleagues have created, bookmarked, or linked that are tuned to your clients—ready for them to use when they take their first few steps into the Web.

Think *basic*. Don't give students more information than they need or can handle at that moment. Even if you don't remember all young users and what you have previously told or shown them, you can easily tell how well-versed they are with the Web by observing how they navigate and conduct their searches. Your goal should be to have those students coming back to the library again and again, and each time they come in, you can share a little more about finding things and evaluating them.

You also have to bear in mind the age appropriateness of your approach in teaching young people using the Web. Particularly with younger children, third and fourth graders, keep it simple, very simple, by giving them very specific instructions without getting into too much of the *how* and *why* things work or do not work. It's more important to map out something for them first so they can feel comfortable using the search tools available locally or on the Web. You should let them think of the search terms and type them in, but you will need to stay close at hand to help them through each step if needed. When they gain some confidence, then, little by little, you can give them more information about how to fine-tune their searches.

For older students, fifth grade and up, explain to them the works behind the search tools. The added value of this approach is to let them know that you, as a professional information retriever, know something that they themselves might not know and, thus, they can trust your instruction even more. Some older elementary students or middle school students feel that they are more Net- or Web-savvy than their librarians are. It is always useful to keep a step ahead of these youngsters and once in a while dazzle them with a piece of information that they do not already know.

Simple Instruction Methods

There are many ways that people have tried to teach young people how to "work" the Web. Designing and photocopying a simple flyer or creating a clear Web page to guide young people through the quirks of your specific local system—or the Web in general—can be very helpful.

Another quick-and-dirty way of teaching them how to search on the Web is to design a local Web page (see chapter 4) that includes basic skills information presented attractively. Attractiveness is crucial. As Angela Weiler, instruction librarian at State University of New York mentioned in her e-mail to us:

> The brighter the colors and the wilder the graphics, the more they liked it and the longer they stuck with it. They absorbed more of the information when it held their attention with color or movement.

We do not encourage truckloads of animated GIF files or huge graphic files, for that will lengthen the wait time for the pages to load up. Too much color and movement might risk losing your young patrons' attention or interest, but we do encourage a balance of good layout and graphic design to make the pages, especially the instructional pages, readable and enjoyable.

Instructional Local Pages

Design a local Web page not only to gather links but also to include a section of "touring" the Web so that first time or novice users can use it as a guide when they want to learn at their own pace. Look at Ms. Spider's Guide to the Internet on the Baltimore County Public Library site for an example at http://www.bcpl.lib.md.us/kidspage/familyfun/spider.html. You also can take a look at some instructional curriculum about using search tools in the webliography under the Training section.

Jamie McKenzie, writing about training methods, said

> As I have worked on research models for schools during the past three years, I continue to see the need for a well-planned progression from structured research experiences (highly guided) towards those calling for great independence.[1]

A sample of very basic Web skills designed and used on the Web is the World Wide Web Workbook of the Franklin Institute Science Museum at http://www.fi.edu/primer/newprimer/. The text is simple and easy to follow. The stages of skills and progress are well-organized. We suggest modeling your "tour" on the organization of this site and incorporating attractive designs for your young users. This site only teaches about the physical skills and not logical skills needed to find things on the Web.

It's always a good idea to create a page with links to the search engines that you and other library staff members are comfortable using and rely upon. (See figure 6.1, or to see a live example, visit the Dalton Middle School's library page at http://www.dalton.org/groups/libraries/MSLIB/

Figure 6.1   Sample Library Search Tools Page

Web Search Tools

Search Engines, <u>Meta-Search Engines</u> and <u>Subject Indexes/Directories</u>

Search Engines

<u>AltaVista</u> | <u>Excite</u> | <u>HotBot</u> | <u>Infoseek</u> | <u>Lycos</u> | <u>Magellan</u> | <u>Northern Light</u> | <u>Open Text</u> | <u>Web Crawler</u>

net_search.html.) Most young users tend to click on the default Net Search button in Netscape Navigator or Communicator. They usually fail to notice that each time they are taken to that page, they are actually using a randomly chosen search tool (chosen randomly, that is, from a small list of search tools that have paid Netscape large amounts of money to be on the list). If you can, deactivate the tool bar. (In version 3.0x, choose Options, then highlight Show Directory Buttons; in version 4.0x, choose View, then Hide Navigation Tool Bar.). If you can't do so or think that the Net Search page from Netscape is a good way for children to do their searches, then you *must* draw their attention to the fact that there are a few search tools they can choose from on that page. They should also understand the tips and help hints of the tool they are about to use. You might attach a very short text note in a larger font size to remind young users to read the Help or Tips section on each search engine if they have trouble finding good information.

Do not expect to be the students' only and ultimate instructor in research skills. View the opportunity to help them be more Web-search savvy as something extra you can do for them. The basic logical thinking skills should be something that they have to acquire over time.

Do not be frustrated if a child cannot understand the process after one brief training session. Also, try avoiding giving too much "education" at once. Do not stretch a reference session into a research lecture course. Remember, when we use reference books, sometimes we only have time and opportunity to show them a certain topic is covered from page 35 to page 38 in a book, "Wal-Mart" style. We don't typically have the time to get into the "how a reference book is researched and published and how you can better your research skills if you listen to me and learn how to look things up" discussion.

If you have the luxury (or are required) to plan training sessions for your patrons and students, the following sections offer some advice.

Web Workshops and Activities

Either in a public library or in a school library, you can offer workshops to train young patrons in the skills they need to surf the Net. Some basic elements to keep in mind include the following:

Make the sessions as relevant, lively, and fun as possible. Look for things that really will draw young people's attention. Once, for a workshop on using the Web as an information resource during the Olympic games, we had the Olympics site ready on a bookmark. We asked beginning students to find how many gold, silver, and bronze medals certain countries had won. All of them enjoyed it, and they competed to see who could find the information fastest. At another training in an inner-city middle school, when we thought we were losing a couple of girls in the back row, we asked one of them what she would like to find out more about. "[The hip-hop artist] Mase," she said, in a tone that suggested that someone as cool as Mase couldn't have anything to do with this boring stuff. So we went into HotBot and found three Mase sites, all the while showing the class how to use a search engine and read the results, and we had the girl and her friends' undivided attention for the next fifteen minutes. "Can I get those URLs from you?" she asked us three times.

Make the sessions as compact as possible but without losing essential details. Include just enough explanation that students will understand what they're doing a little more clearly. When you're in front of a class of beginners, it's always a good idea to talk for two minutes or so about what the Internet is. We like to say that "Bringing up a Web site in your browser is like your computer making a long distance phone call to another computer—except it's a free call. Lots of times you don't know which computer you're calling, or where it is; it might be across the street or eight thousand miles away. But the URL you type into the Location box is the area code and the phone number. Remember," we tell them, "the

Figure 6.2   Graphical Conception of
Net Connections

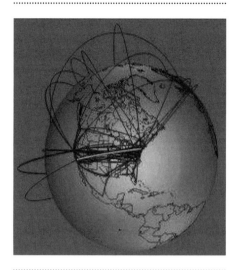

SOURCE: An Atlas of Cyberspaces available
at http://www.cybergeography.org/atlas/
geographic.html.

Internet is made up of thousands of computers wired together, just like the phone system is millions of connected telephones." We like to show them one of the many graphic representations of the worldwide connectivity of the Net like the one in figure 6.2.

When something does not work right, turn the problem into an educational element. Remind the students that the Web or a certain searching strategy may not always be perfect. The always-reliable site you so much want to show them may turn up 404 (not found) or be missing its domain name server entry (the host machine is either out of service or no longer exists) one fateful morning. The usually fast-loading site may have only half its graphics showing after three very long minutes have passed. "Oh, well," we tell them, "that's the Web; it's always changing, and sometimes it's really busy and slow. Let's find something else."

If you want to show young people how to use search tools, stick to one or two—HotBot and Yahoo, perhaps—to begin with. Find out from the teacher which topics students might need to locate, and customize your demonstration search to their immediate needs. Ask students what they need to find, and do the search with them. You should bring up the search tool's box and ask them, "What words might you use to find sites on that? Should we do it as a phrase or as separate words?" Use the words they suggest, and be sure to show them how many hits their search brings up. "Let's see; we put in 'Civil War' as a phrase and we get 186,822 hits. How could we get fewer hits?" Stress that more is not better. ("Do you want to look through 186,000 sites? I don't!"), and that no matter how sophisticated a search engine might be, the deciding factor in finding good and useful materials lies with the user's abilities. Stress that forming a query precisely is more important than any other search skill. You should also demonstrate the power of synonyms and related words: "As well as 'biomes,' should we try 'habitats' or specific biomes? How about the words 'desert,' 'fauna,' and 'habitat,' as separate words rather than as a phrase?"

This type of flexibility in your instruction only comes after you have used the Web and searching tools fluently and freely for a while. Before instructing young patrons, you have to use the Web a lot; there is just no shortcut around it.

Example of Public Library Internet Workshops and Activities

Family Internet Workshop, New York Public Lirary

At the Central Children's Room at New York Public Library, staff give a workshop on searching the Internet. The approach is family-oriented. Here is the text of a handout that goes along with the workshop.

Exploring the Internet as a Family

A program for children ages 7 to 12 and their caregivers offered by the Central Children's Room, Donnell Library Center.

Pre-registration is required. Space is limited to 10 people.

The information superhighway has a lot to offer. Sometimes there's so much out there it can be overwhelming. The trick is to figure out how to sift through the Web for the sites that are interesting and cool—like driving to the beach without getting lost or breaking down. We're going to show you how to get out of the driveway and on to the highway—how to find what you want, how to decide if it is worth anything, and some interesting side trips you can make.

A good place to start is On-Lion, the New York Public Library's page for kids. This page has links to all kinds of informative and fun sites as well as booklists and information on events going on in the Library for kids.

http://www.nypl.org/branch/kids/onlion.html

"Yahooligans" is a great place to start looking for information when you don't already know where to go. This search engine is especially designed for kids, with topics like homework answers and hobbies.

http://www.yahooligans.com

If you can't always go online, there are plenty of books that help explain computers and the Internet and contain lots of cool sites to explore when you get to the computer. Here are some suggestions:

- *Computer Dictionary for Kids . . . and Their Parents* by Jami Lynne Borman. J 004.03 B
- *The Internet* by Kerry Cochrane. J 004.67 C
- *Internet for Kids!* by Ted Pedersen and Francis Moss. J 004.67 P
- *The Internet Kids Yellow Pages* by Jean Armour Polly. J 025.04 P
- *Kids On-Line* by Marian Salzman and Robert Pondiscio. J 004.69 S

There's a lot to discover on the information superhighway. Have fun—and drive safely!

The staff trainers always keep the session in the confines of the library's own children's page. They show what sites are chosen and linked under each category and demonstrate simple searches using Yahooligans. You can see how this workshop is kept *local* and compact. The session lasts only about 30 to 45 minutes for a small group of up to 10 people. It is a one-time deal because most public libraries can only offer this type of arrangement and not an involved series of sessions.

Bedford (Indiana) Public Library Internet Workshop

Another workshop is offered at the Bedford Public Library, Bedford, Indiana. The workshop lasts one hour and is a one-time deal, too. This workshop is offered to children and parents/adults (a child under 10 must be accompanied by an adult). The workshop includes how to reserve time in advance for Internet computers, printing cost, what is allowed and what is not allowed on the library computers, where to find computer books, and general Internet navigation and printing instructions.

Each Bedford Public Library Internet workshop attendee receives a booklet, bookmark, and sticker. (See figure 6.3.) The ten-page booklet includes the library Internet use policy, a short introduction to the Internet and the World Wide Web, pages devoted to using Netscape, and the basics of Net searching. The author of this booklet recommends Net Search but does point out that there are several choices on that one page. A concise and accurate explanation of printing in Netscape Navigator is included as well. Two more pages are devoted to some sites of interest; it's always good to send young people and parents home with a bookmark or flyer filled with the library's own Web site URL as well as some URLs of "can't miss" Web sites elsewhere. If you have a YPWRC, this URL should always be the first URL in any list you publish. Offer not a list of "links sites" but a list of sites with real content to share in a topic area or at a grade level.

Canton (Michigan) Public Library Course and Scavenger Hunt

Canton Public Library has a "Cyber Kids" Room with seven networked PCs. Before young people are allowed to use them, they must take a quick course (about fifteen minutes long) on how to use a browser, navigate the library's site, and use the library's YPWRC. Children are told the library's Web station use policies, and after agreeing to follow them, receive a Cyber Kids card that allows them to sign up for time slots on the PCs.

Figure 6.3   Bedford Public Library's Internet Workshop Materials

Aside from this quick course, Canton Public Library offers a fun way for young people to get some practice using the Web in ways they otherwise might not—an Internet scavenger hunt. Here the Cyber Kids must use the sites in the library's YPWRC to answer trivia questions to solve a riddle, such as "What kind of dog does President Clinton own?" Wendy Woltjer, who creates the Internet Scavenger Hunts, says that her favorite was "a nifty one all about bears for our Summer Reading Program in 1997, and several libraries in the area pointed to it from their home pages." (See figures 6.4 and 6.5.)

Multnomah County (Oregon) Library

Other libraries and schools have also made use of the Internet scavenger hunt as either a training opportunity or a program. In the Multnomah County Library, combination library catalog and Web scavenger hunts have been featured events at several of the young teen sleepover programs the library has held in the spring and summer. The librarians typically break the young teens into groups of three or four, give each group a sheet of

Figure 6.4   Canton Public Library's Scavenger Hunt Resources

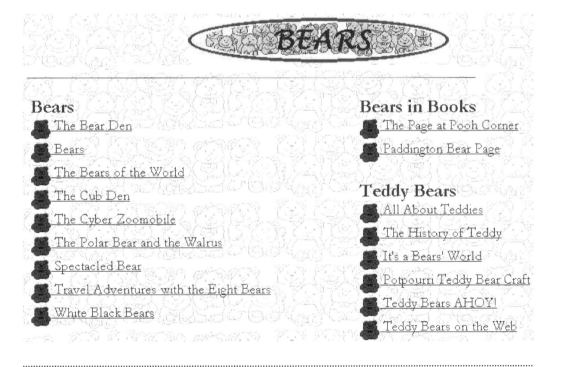

Figure 6.5 Canton Public Library's Scavenger Hunt Questions

LET'S GO ON A BEAR HUNT!

Find the answers to the following bear questions using our BearSite* to solve this riddle:

Why didn't the grizzly walk on the gravel road?

$\overline{1}\ \overline{2}\ \overline{3}\quad \overline{4}\ \overline{5}\ \overline{6}\quad \overline{7}\ \overline{8}\ \overline{9}\ \overline{10}\quad \overline{11}\ \overline{12}\ \overline{13}\ \overline{14}$!

*http://metronet.lib.mi.us/CANT/YOUTH/current.html

1. Which bears sometimes carry their young on their back?

$\underline{}\ \underline{}\ \underline{}\ \underline{2}\ \underline{}\ \underline{12}\ \underline{}\ \underline{}\ \underline{}$

2. What is another name for the grizzly bear?

$\underline{7}\ \underline{}\ \underline{}\ \underline{}\ \underline{}\ \underline{13}\ \underline{}\ \underline{}$

3. How many kinds of bears are there?

$\underline{}\ \underline{}\ \underline{}\ \underline{4}\ \underline{14}$

4. Which U.S. President is the "teddy" bear named after?

$\underline{}\ \underline{}\ \underline{}\ \underline{6}\ \underline{}\ \underline{}\quad \underline{}\ \underline{}\ \underline{}\ \underline{1}\ \underline{}\ \underline{}$

5. In the Winter, many bears take long naps in their dens. This is called $\underline{}\ \underline{}\ \underline{2}\ \underline{}\ \underline{}\ \underline{}\ \underline{5}\ \underline{}$.

6. Who wrote Winnie the Pooh?

$\underline{}\ \overset{.}{\underline{9}}\ \underline{}\ \underline{}\ \underline{}\ \underline{3}$

7. Which bear is the smallest of all?

$\underline{}\ \underline{1}\ \underline{}\ \underline{}\ \underline{8}\ \underline{}$

8. Which bear's scientific name is "Ursus americanus?"

$\underline{}\ \underline{}\ \underline{}\ \underline{10}\ \underline{}\ \underline{}\quad \underline{}\ \underline{}\ \underline{}\ \underline{13}\ \underline{}$

twenty questions, and award prizes (gift certificates donated by a local bookstore) to the team that answers the most questions correctly in one hour (and that hour goes quickly). Sample questions range from "How many different Tori Amos CD titles does the library system own?" to "How many colors are there on the flag of Kenya? What colors are they?" It's easy to see how such a scavenger hunt can help young users develop their skills in navigating the library catalog and the Web in a painless way.

Web Scavenger Hunt Tips

If you would like to run a scavenger hunt on the Web, following are a few tips:

- Require that all answers must come from the library's site and YPWRC. This is a great opportunity to get young users familiar with the sites you have assembled for their use. Choose questions from sites that are particularly appealing. This requirement also discourages "wandering" on the Web.

- If a question is library-related, choose one that will—you hope—cause the young "hunter" to say, "Ah! I didn't know that." Never stop advertising how great the library is.

- Require that the young people write down the URL of the page on which they found the answer, in case there are any questions.

- Mix easier questions with harder ones. You would be surprised; a question that seems easy to you can completely stump an eighth grader, and one you think would be tough might be quick and easy for the same student.

Planned Lessons

In planned lessons, the librarian instructor has the luxury to work gradually with students from the basic elements to more-complicated issues. All the points mentioned in the previous sections are valid. However, here, you can really use your imagination and creativity to work with teachers in developing a curriculum that will help children develop more-sophisticated searching skills.

Arthropods on the Web

We will show you in detail one example of a three-week training session we did for 100 fifth graders at the Dalton School in New York City.

Note: Macintosh computers are used in this training program, so there is only one mouse button. This is a locally customized lesson that might not work in your library. For example, the printing process and saving of the text process is needed in this particular school because it uses Macs and LaserJet printers that do not support the Preview function. Your students might not all have access to an Internet terminal with enough time during your class period to finish the assigned project, and they might have to go to a local public library. There they might encounter new restrictions. You might need to know some of the characteristics of your local public library computers and work that information into your lesson plan.

You have to design these lessons carefully to meet the needs and restrictions that your students have and face. Of course, on-the-spot reinforcement in the midst of an assignment is always important because this is the time when a child really needs something from the Net, and the impression he or she receives will be the strongest.

First Session

To illustrate and explain some basic concepts of Boolean Searching Logic, we use a visual aid. On five pieces of square poster board (1 foot by 1 foot), we paste a bunch of (seemingly) randomly placed shapes in several colors. Green triangles, red triangles, orange triangles, green squares, red squares, orange squares, etc., in two difference sizes—big and small.

We show these boards to the students and ask the students to imagine multiplying this board a million times. Then we explain to them that this is more or less a "visualization" of what the information on the Web is like: a lot of pieces of information—practically unorganized.

We ask them if it is economic or even possible to physically pick out all the green triangles. It is clear to them that it will be time-consuming and hard to do, even if it is theoretically possible. Then we go on to have a discussion about the strength of computer programs to help them find information more rapidly. Here we stress the point that *we* are the thinkers behind all the searches, and that is why we have to learn to construct intelligent and effective searches to retrieve relevant and useful information.

Once this concept is established, we write two words on a black board: green triangle. Ask them to point out the pieces on the poster boards that this little robot we call a computer program or a search engine will bring back to us according to this command.

They soon realize that since the robot cannot intelligently understand that green triangle means something very specific in our mind, it will give us all the pieces that are green and all the pieces that are triangular.

Here is where we introduce the quotation marks operator. We explain that if we put down our request like this:

"green triangle"

the robot will bring back only "green triangles."

The next step is to introduce the concepts of AND and OR.

We write on the black (white) board:

"green triangle" AND / OR "red square"

Students are asked to guess which of these two "operators" will bring back *more* results. The common answer is AND.

Out of the five poster boards, three of them contain both green triangles and red squares. One of them contains only green triangles and no red squares and the remaining one contains only red squares but no green triangles. Presented with these five "documents," they soon realize that with the operator AND, only three documents will be retrieved, but all five will fit our requirements if we have used OR.

Then the concept NOT is introduced. Using the five poster boards, it is easy for them to see the function demonstrated by

"green triangle" NOT "red square"

After this, we show them the parentheses operators on the board to illustrate the difference between

("green triangle" OR "red square") AND big
("green triangle" AND "red square") AND small

(You must make sure that at least one of the five boards contains only small pieces or big pieces.) That's enough information for them to think about before next session. No actual Web searches are conducted during this first session.

Second Session

We refresh their memory on the basic few operators learned in the first session by presenting the poster boards one more time and doing a few Boolean exercises. Then we use the research project that they are working on to form some queries on the board. They are researching the life cycle, diet, reproduction, habitats, and some other information on various arthropods (ants, spiders, lobsters, silkworms, butterflies, etc.).

The following is a handout for each student to help him or her get familiar with one search engine that supports Boolean search strategy. Before giving students the handout and letting them go online to do their searches, each point is illustrated on the board.

How to form an *effective* search using www.HotBot.com and Boolean phrases:

First: Go to the HotBot homepage by typing http://www.hotbot.com/ at the Net Sites space on the top part of Netscape.

Second: At the Look For (which shows "all the words") space, click on the *down* arrow once to pull down the dialog box. Choose *Boolean phrase* by moving your mouse pointer down and highlight it.

Third: At the white space next to the Search button, type in your words to search. Example phrases:

(spider OR spiders) AND (habitat OR "life cycle")

Substitute your Arthropod here, such as:

(grasshopper OR grasshoppers) AND (habitat OR "life cycle")

Or, if you are looking for information about its diet and "life span," you can type

(butterfly OR butterflies) AND diet AND "life span"

Fourth: a. Click on the Search button once.
b. Wait.
c. The results will be returned ten at a time.
d. Read the short description under each numbered link to the site.
e. Decide whether to click on the link to investigate the site.
f. Click on the link to a site you want to read.
g. Read and see if there is information useful to your report.
h. For today—do not print anything out. You *can* copy down the URL (the Web address) for a particularly useful or interesting site.

Third Session

The students receive another handout and demonstration of some additional information.

1. If you find that *too* many results are returned and most of the top ones share similar or same elements that are not useful to your project, you should use NOT to eliminate them. For example, in searching for information on ANTS, you see a lot of pages from pest control companies selling pesticides. Your new query might look like this:

(ant OR ants) AND diet AND ("life cycle" OR "life span") NOT "pest control"

2. Since our printers do not support the Netscape function for Preview of the pages you would like to print out and take home, you should print *only* the first page of the document to keep track of the URL and the title of the page. Please open a text editor (Word) and copy and paste *only* the part of text you need onto a blank page and then print that page out.

3. To print just the one image you want:

    a. Click and hold down the mouse button for a few seconds on the picture you want to view or print; a pull-down menu will appear.

    b. Move to highlight the choice of "Open this image." You will then see *only* the picture on a page of its own.

    c. Now you can press Print to print this picture.

4. Since Web Pages on the Internet are very recent inventions and people only have just started using them as research resources, there is not yet one definite way to cite a Web page. All the computers in the middle school library are set up so there will be information on the print out to show you where you've gotten the information. It might not always be easy or even possible to determine who the author is . . . but try your best to find out who it is. Looking at a site's home page will often be helpful. Check especially for a date. The date cited should be when the file was last updated.

Burka, Lauren P. "A Hypertext History of Multi-User Dimensions." MUD History. http://www.ccs.neu.edu/home/lpb/mud-history.html (5 Dec. 1994).

The material in quotes is the title of the actual page you have cited. The unquoted title is the title of the home page of the material you are citing. The date is whatever date is cited in the document (often listed as "last update"). The author of the page is usually listed at the bottom of each Web page as the person to contact.

What if you can't find the date or the author? The one crucial element you *must* have is the URL (http://www . . . etc.) If you can't find a last update date, put in *(accessed 10 Feb. 1998).*

Fourth Session

This is an evaluation session for you, the librarian instructor. Give each student a simple research project to bring up one selected page that fits the query. Have each student print out the first page of the document and selected paragraphs.

It will benefit your young patrons and students tremendously if you can show them that patience, persistence, calmness, and a bit of creative flexibility usually pay off.

The Last Word

Helping young people develop their information literacy skills is essential to making sense of the world at the beginning of the twenty-first century. Technology and media will become increasingly subtle and complex as the years go by, and the student who will do best is the student who is sensitive to subtle clues in all media. You can make yourself essential to the students making their way through all these media if you do your best to stay alongside them in technological knowledge while sharing the traditional talents and skills of the librarian. These include a deep knowledge of language and its nuances, the ability to put concepts and ideas into order, and the ability to hunt down information from the best—and the strangest—sources. Good luck!

Note

1. Jamie McKenzie, "The Internet as Curriculum," *From Now On: The Educational Technology Journal,* available at http://fromnowon.org/jan97/curriculum.html.

Information Literacy

Standard 1: The student who is information literate accesses information efficiently and effectively.

Standard 2: The student who is information literate evaluates information critically and competently.

Standard 3: The student who is information literate uses information accurately and creatively.

Independent Learning

Standard 4: The student who is an independent learner is information literate and pursues information related to personal interests.

Standard 5: The student who is an independent learner is information literate and appreciates literature and other creative expressions of information.

Standard 6: The student who is an independent learner is information literate and strives for excellence in information seeking and knowledge generation.

Social Responsibility

Standard 7: The student who contributes positively to the learning community and to society is information literate and recognizes the importance of information to a democratic society.

Standard 8: The student who contributes positively to the learning community and to society is information literate and practices ethical behavior in regard to information and information technology.

Standard 9: The student who contributes positively to the learning community and to society is information literate and participates effectively in groups to pursue and generate information.

Webliography

Following is a list of Web sites arranged roughly in the order of topics presented in this book. "Acc." in a citation means "date accessed." For the most current version of this list, check our site at http://www.igloo-press.com/webreference/webliography.html.

General Information and Discussion

1997 National Survey of Public Libraries and the Internet: Summary Results
Office for Information Technology Policy, ALA. 1997.
http://www.ala.org/oitp/research/plcon97sum/index.html

> A press release and a survey result reporting the 1997 Internet access situation in U.S. public libraries. Read the survey using Acrobat Reader.

A Beginner's Guide to URLs
The MOSAIC team, National Center for Supercomputing Applications.
Acc. 14 Mar. 1998.
http://www.ncsa.uiuc.edu/demoweb/url-primer.html

> Clear descriptions of several types of URLs.

Evaluation Rubrics for Websites
Loogootee Elementary West, Loogootee, Ind. June 1997,
updated 23 Mar. 1998.
http://www.siec.k12.in.us/~west/online/eval.htm

> Site-evaluation forms for primary, intermediate, and secondary grades.

From Now On: Educational Technology for Schools
Jamie McKenzie. 1995– .
http://fromnowon.org/

> An e-zine published by Jamie McKenzie, an author, educator, and consultant to several state departments of education and school districts. Offers a huge quantity of thoughtful essays about technology in schools.

Internet Basics
CyberU. Southern Regional High School, Manahawkin, N.J.
Acc. 14 Mar. 1998.
http://dune.srhs.k12.nj.us/WWW/contents.htm

> Practical and short discussions about all aspects of the Net including random surfing, bookmarks, search engines, and evaluating Web sites. Its target audience is high school students.

Internet Guides
Neil Enns. 1995.
http://www.brandonu.ca/~ennsnr/Resources/guides.html

> A list of links to all aspects of the Internet; may be a little overwhelming.

IPL Especially for Librarians: Internet for Libraries
The Internet Public Library. 13 Mar. 1998.
http://www.ipl.org/svcs/internet.html

> Practical resources focused on Internet skills for librarians and Internet policies and implementations for libraries accompanied by many examples.

IPL Especially for Librarians: Organizing the Web
The Internet Public Library. 23 Jan. 1998.
http://www.ipl.org/svcs/organizing.html

> Methods to organize the Web promoted by various organizations and educational institutes, with short comments and a link to each example.

SLMQ (School Library Media Quarterly) Online
American Association of School Librarians, ALA. 1998– .
http://www.ala.org/aasl/SLMQ.

> The official journal of the American Association of School Librarians.

Selected Search Tools

Search Engines for Pinpointed Searching

AltaVista
http://www.altavista.digital.com

> Many searchers' favorite tool, with non-English language and full Boolean capabilities.

Excite
http://www.excite.com

Best for broad, general searches; Power Search feature allows an easy Boolean search with no knowledge of Boolean terminology.

HotBot
http://www.hotbot.com

From the publishers of *Wired* magazine, excellent search engine that is as psychedelic as they come. SuperSearch allows extremely sophisticated searches with no Boolean knowledge. Our recommendation.

Infoseek
http://www.infoseek.com

Like most commercial search engines, offers many business and sales-oriented features. Engine software very accurate in tests. Also has a Kids and Families area sponsored by Disney.

Lycos
http://www.lycos.com

Good tools for complex searches, including searches for multimedia files and Usenet newsgroup messages.

Northern Light
http://www.nlsearch.com/

A comparatively new and powerful search engine. Aside from the usual Web database, also houses journal articles that can be individually purchased at a very reasonable rate.

Metasearch Tools for Simple Searches

DogPile
http://www.dogpile.com

Depending on your taste, either the best-named or worst-named search tool. Searches Web, Usenet newsgroups, news services, and ftp sites.

Inference Find
http://www.inference.com/infind/

Specializes in speed, and is fast.

MetaCrawler
http://www.metcrawler.com

> A nicely customizable metasearch tool. Can search by continent or by domain type.

Commercial Subject Directories for Broad Overviews of Topics

Ask Jeeves for Kids
http:::/www..ajkids.com

> A filtered subject directory for young people, with frames to discourage "wandering" on the Web. Young people can ask questions in natural language. Offers "suggestions" automatically, although not all are relevant to the question asked.

Magellan Internet Guide
http://www.mckinley.com

> Reviewers have annotated sites, given them star ratings, and marked safe-for-kids sites with a green light.

Planet K–12
http://planetk-12.planetsearch.com/

> Part of the PlanetSearch search engine/directory; offers a choice between a general Web search and an education sites database search. Targeted at educators, not students.

Yahoo
http://www.yahoo.com

> The number 1 search tool worldwide at present, although not the best for all searches. Good for browsing. Strong regional and international presence but very commercial.

Yahooligans
http://www.yahooligans.com

> Good for young people to use as a browsing tool. A subset of the Yahoo database from which "adult" and "questionable" sites have been removed, although the strong commercial orientation remains.

Specialized Search Tools

BigYellow
http://www.bigyellow.com/

Find Web sites and contact information for businesses, associations, and other institutions.

International Lyric Server
http://www.lyrics.ch/

Find the lyrics to more than 70,000 songs, including folk songs and current chart-toppers.

Switchboard
http://www.switchboard.com

A search service to find people and businesses in the United States, including addresses, phone numbers, and maps.

WhoWhere
http://www.whowhere.com

A search tool designed for finding people, including their addresses, phone numbers, and e-mail addresses.

Search Tips and Search Engine Comparison

The 7 Habits of Highly Effective Surfers, Plus 3 for Total Control Freaks
Daniel A. Tauber and Brenda Kienan. C|Net. 16 Feb. 1998.
http://www.cnet.com/Content/Features/Dlife/Habits/index.html

An amusing and informative article.

Beyond Surfing: Tools and Techniques for Searching the Web
Kathleen Webster and Kathryn Paul. *Information Technology.* 16 Jan. 1996– .
http://magi.com/~mmelick/it96jan.htm

An article about search tools with a lot of sites listed and a webliography of other similar articles on the Web.

The Building and Maintenance of Robot Based Internet Search Services: A Review of Current Indexing and Data Collection Methods
T. Koch, A. Ardö, A. Brümmer, and S. Lundberg. 26 Sept. 1996.
http://www.ub2.lu.se/desire/radar/reports/D3.11/

> An extensive technical study of how search tools work on the Web.

Choose the Best Engine for Your Purpose
Debbie Abilock. 8 Aug. 1996, rev. 1 July 1997.
http://www.nueva.pvt.k12.ca.us/~debbie/library/research/adviceengine.html

> An interesting approach—this page offers a chart to show the search tool corresponding with each type of informational need. Most valuable is the analysis of "What to do when your search produces no results" at the bottom half of this page.

Eight Internet Search Engines Compared
Richard Einer Peterson. *First Monday.* 1997.
http://www.firstmonday.dk/issues/issue2_2/peterson/index.html

> Evaluates AltaVista, Excite, HotBot, Infoseek guide, Lycos, Open Text, Ultra, and WebCrawler.

Hints & Tips for Searching the Internet at Classroom Connect
Classroom Connect. Acc. 14 Mar. 1998.
http://www.classroomconnect.com/searching/searchingfaq.html

> A short document that addresses all the points covered in this book. Excellent to use as an example when creating a tips flyer for users.

Lost in Cyberspace
David Drake. *New Scientist.* 28 June 1997.
http://www.keysites.com/keysites/networld/lost.html

> A short but succinct article on Web searching.

Search Engine Watch
Danny Sullivan, editor. Mechlermedia. 1996–1998.
http://www.searchenginewatch.com/

> Recommended if you're interested in how search engines tick; helps all Web users understand search engines and how they operate.

Search Engines: What They Are, How They Work, and Practical Suggestions for Getting the Most Out of Them
Bruce Grossan. Webreference. Rev. 21 Feb. 1997.
http://www.webreference.com/content/search/

> A clear and well-designed page on search engine basics and comparisons.

The Search Is Over: The Search-Engine Secrets of the Pros by Adam Page
Adam Page. ZDNet. 1997.
http://www4.zdnet.com/pccomp/features/fea1096/sub2.html

> A very good article about search engines, search tips, and comparison. A "must read."

Searching the Internet
Clifford Lynch. *Scientific American.* Mar. 1997.
http://www.sciam.com/0397issue/0397lynch.html

> Subtitled: Combining the skills of the librarian and the computer scientist may help organize the anarchy of the Internet.

The Spider's Apprentice
Linda Barlow. Monash Information Services. 14 Jan. 98.
http://www.monash.com/spidap.html

> An excellent review of Boolean searching techniques.

Understanding WWW Search Tools by Jian Liu, at IUB Libraries
Jian Liu. Indiana University–Bloomington. Sept. 1996.
http://www.indiana.edu/~librcsd/search/

> Comments, tips, and facts about search tools.

The Web Robots FAQ . . .
Martijn Koster. WebCrawler. Acc. 14 Mar. 1998.
http://info.webcrawler.com/mak/projects/robots/faq.html

> For those who are *really* curious as to how robots work in the information-retrieval process on the Web.

Web Searching
Internet Public Library. 18 Jan. 1997.
http://www.ipl.org/ref/websearching.html

> A short page indicating the pros and cons of several major search tools on the Web.

Where to Find Anything on the Net
Andrew J. Leonard. C|Net. 1997.
http://www.cnet.com/Content/Reviews/Compare/Search/

> Nineteen search engines and metasearch engines listed, described, and compared. Tips offered, too.

HTML, Site Design, and Site Maintenance

Carl Davis's—HTML Editor Reviews
Carl Davis. Rev. 22 Sept. 97.
http://www.webcommando.com/editrev/index.html

> List of HTML editors, reviews, and comparison charts to guide readers through the many choices of HTML authoring packages.

Doctor HTML—from Imagiware
Thomas Tongue and Imagiware, Inc. 1995–1997.
http://www2.imagiware.com:80/RxHTML/htdocs/single.html

> Free online links checker that allows you to customize things to check—links, document structure, and spelling.

Dr. Watson
Addy and Assoc. Rev. 6 May 1998.
http://watson.addy.com/

> Links checker that verifies up to fifty links per page and returns results on the Web.

Home Pages: Homely or Handsome?
Online Internet Institute. Acc. 14 Mar. 1998.
http://www.teleport.com/~janetm/oii/home.html

> A practical checklist for anyone preparing to launch a Web site.

International and Special Characters in HTML
Paul Hoffman. Proper Publishing. Taken and reformatted from IETF RFC 1866, "HyperText Markup Language—2.0." Acc. 12 May 1998.
http://www.proper.com/www/intchar.html

> A handy reference for all Web authors.

Linking to Community Data for Your Library's Web Pages
Jenny Hawk. Rev. 3 Sept. 1997.
http://sashimi.wwa.com/~jayhawk/locallinks.html

> A good introduction to how to construct a local-information page. Although oriented toward adult services, concepts are still useful in children's and YA work.

Links Checkers
The Web Developer's Virtual Library. Acc. 14 Mar. 1998.
http://Stars.com/Authoring/HTML/Validation/Links.html

> A list of links checkers available to validate links on your Web site.

NCSA HTML Resources
The National Center for Supercomputing Applications. University of Illinois at Urbana–Champaign. Rev. 17 Feb. 1998.
http://www.ncsa.uiuc.edu/Indices/Resources/html-resources.html

> A comprehensive collection of tutorials from the very basics of Web authoring to the advanced level.

NetMechanic
Monte Sano Software. 1996.
http://www.netmechanic.com/

> A free Web product that allows you to submit your directories and files to validate the links on those pages. Response mailed to your e-mail address.

Web Developer's Virtual Library
Alan and Lucy Richmond. Updated constantly. Acc. 12 May 1998.
http://www.stars.com/

> For any Web developer, this one has it all.

Writing HTML Documents
SingNet WWW Team. One World. 6 Feb. 1996.
http://oneworld.wa.com/htmldev/devpage/dev-page1.html

> A page of links to Web authoring pages arranged in four categories—beginner, advanced, fancy, and HTML standards.

Training and Information Literacy

BCK2SKOL Lessons: A New Class on the Net for Librarians with Little or No Net Experience

Ellen Chamberlain. Board of Trustees of the University of South Carolina. 1997, rev. 9 Mar. 1998.
http://www.sc.edu/bck2skol/fall/fall.html

> Thirty-session Web classroom designed for librarians and library staff—but can definitely be customized for teaching young users about the Web.

Citing Electronic Resources

The Internet Public Library. 19 Mar. 1998.
http://www.ipl.org/ref/QUE/FARQ/netciteFARQ.html

> Citing Web resources, still a morphing process, but contains pointers to several suggestion sites.

Citing Internet Addresses

Classroom Connect. 1997.
http://www.gsn.org/web/_lib/_biblio/CitingNe.htm

> From Classroom Connect, a list of structures and examples in citing resources from e-mail to http sites.

Exploring the World-Wide Web

Brad Cahoon. University of Georgia Center for Continuing Education. Rev. 2 July 1997.
http://www.gactr.uga.edu/exploring/index.html

> A seven-part Web-based tutorial that can assist anyone who wishes to conduct Web workshops. Covers software, hardware, searching, and authoring.

Filamentality

San Diego State University/Pacific Bell Fellows Applications Design Team/ Wired Learning. Rev. 1 Aug. 1997.
http://www.kn.pacbell.com/wired/fil

> Designed to help teachers and librarians help students explore the Net and evaluate what makes a worthwhile Web site while creating new learning-oriented pages.

How to Help Someone Use a Computer
Phil Agre, editor. *The Network Observer* 1, no. 5 (1994).
http://weber.ucsd.edu/~pagre/tno/may-1994.html#how

> Many helpful and realistic points to follow that can be applied when helping someone use the Net.

Information Literacy and the Net
Bellingham Public Schools, Bellingham, Wash. 23 Oct. 1996.
http://www.bham.wednet.edu/literacy.htm

> Eight-hour staff-development course that emphasizes student investigations as vehicles to explore the information available over the Internet.

The Internet as Curriculum
Jamie McKenzie. *From Now On* 6, no. 4 (Jan. 1997).
http://www.fromnowon.org/~mckenzie/jan97/curriculum.html

> A thoughtful article in *From Now On,* an e-zine for educators.

Searching the 'Net
CyberU. Southern Regional High School, Manahawkin, N.J. Acc. 14 Mar. 1998.
http://dune.srhs.k12.nj.us/WWW/search1.htm

> Seven lessons explain the basics of conducting searches on the Net.

Searching the 'Net: An Online Internet Institute Project
Online Internet Institute. Acc. 14 Mar. 1998.
http://www.teleport.com/~janetm/oii/search.html

> A complete training curriculum that can be adopted and adapted to your needs.

Sink or Swim: Internet Search Tools and Techniques (version 3.0)
Ross Tyner. Okanagan University College Library Home Page, British Columbia, Can. Rev. 27 Apr. 1998.
http://www.sci.ouc.bc.ca/libr/connect96/search.htm

> Another site that might offer some insight and inspiration.

Training the Public in Electronic Services: Tips and Tricks
Tracy Babiasz. Durham County Library, Durham, N.C. Feb. 1998.
http://ils.unc.edu/nclibs/durham/demo/pubtips.html

> A handy checklist for public librarians.

World Wide Web Workbook
The Franklin Institute Science Museum. Acc. 14 Mar. 1998.
http://www.fi.edu/primer/

> A series of Web pages exploring the basic physical skills of using the Web.

Legal Issues, Policies, and Safety

Access to Resources and Services in the School Library Media Program: An Interpretation of the Library Bill of Rights
Office for Information Technology Policy. ALA. 24 Jan. 1996.
http://www.ala.org/oitp/ebillrits.html

> Extends the Library Bill of Rights to cover the rights of users and equity of access issues in school library settings.

Application for Account and Terms and Conditions for Use of Internet
Phil Rose. Academic and Research Computing Services, Florida Tech. Acc. 14 Mar. 1998.
gopher://riceinfo.rice.edu:1170/00/More/Acceptable/fla

> A sample user agreement that can be adopted and adapted.

Child Safety on the Internet
Cranmer Family. Acc. 12 May 1998.
http://www.voicenet.com/~cranmer/censorship.html

> A collection of documents and sites dealing with censorship, freedom of speech, and child safety on the Internet.

Copyright and Legal Issues
Association of Research Libraries. 20–23 Oct. 1992.
gopher://gopher.lib.Virginia.EDU:70/11/alpha/copyright

> A collection of articles dealing with copyright issues on the Web.

Copyright Compliance Instruction
Bellingham Public Schools Board Policy, Bellingham, Wash. Acc. 12 May 1998.
http://www.bham.wednet.edu/copyrght.htm

> An excellent school district copyright policy.

Copyright Law and Internet Resources
Copyright Office, Library of Congress. Acc. 12 May 1998.
gopher://marvel.loc.gov:70/11/copyright

> Copyright issues offered by the gopher server at Library of Congress.

Figuring Out Filters: A Quick Guide to Help Demystify Them
Karen G. Schneider. *School Library Journal Online.* 1 Feb. 1998.
http://www.bookwire.com/SLJ/articles.article$7032

> Renowned filtering expert surveys filters, what they do, and what they
> don't do. Highly recommended.

Rules of the Road
The Benton Foundation. Acc. 12 May 1998.
http://www.benton.org/Library/KickStart/nation.rules.html

> An overview of dealing with intellectual property and copyright issues.
> Recommended.

Good Sample Sites from Library Organizations and School and Public Libraries

ALA 700+ Great Sites: Amazing, Spectacular, Mysterious, Wonderful Web Sites for Kids and the Adults Who Care About Them
ALA. Rev. Apr. 1998.
http://www.ala.org/parentspage/greatsites/

> A collection of sites for kids to age 14 and their parents, caregivers, and
> teachers, with a set of criteria for evaluating the Web sites you find.

ALSC Notable Children's Websites
Association for Library Service to Children. Rev. Jan. 1998.
http://www.ala.org/alsc/ncwc.html

> The ALSC's selection of the best new Web sites for young people
> to age 14.

Ann Arbor District Library Kids' Page
Ann Arbor District Library, Ann Arbor, Mich. Acc. 12 May 1998.
http://www.annarbor.lib.mi.us/kidspg/kidspg2.html

> Resources for children and parents presented in an appealing design.

Baltimore County Public Library Kid's Page
Baltimore County Public Library, Baltimore, Md. Rev. 13 Apr. 1998.
http://www.bcpl.lib.md.us/kidspage/kidspage.html

> Simple, clean, and kid-friendly.

Berkeley Public Library for Kids
Berkeley Public Library, Berkeley, Calif. Rev. 20 Dec. 1997.
http://www.ci.berkeley.ca.us/bpl/kids/index.html

> Search tools, booklists, and homework sites.

Canton Public Library Youth Page
Canton Public Library, Canton, Mich. Acc. 12 May 1998.
http://metronet.lib.mi.us/CANT/youth.html

> Directories to a pleasant mixture of recreational and reference resources.

Internet Public Library
School of Information, University of Michigan, Ann Arbor, Mich.
http://www.ipl.org

> One of the oldest virtual libraries. Produced by a group of enthusiastic information specialists. Exemplary design, organization, and content.

Kathy Schrock's Guide for Educators
Kathy Schrock. Rev. 12 May 1998.
http://www.capecod.net/schrockguide/

> An annotated list of recommended Internet sites "for enhancing curriculum and teacher professional growth." Also useful for library reference work.

Librarians' Index to the Internet
Carole Leita. California State Library. 4 Apr. 1998.
http://sunsite.berkeley.edu/InternetIndex/

> A busy interface but an excellent database. Has a Kids section.

Multnomah County Library Homework Center
Multnomah County Library, Portland, Ore. Acc. 12 May 1998.
http://www.multnomah.lib.or.us/lib/kids/homework/

> Very large library subject directory.

Multnomah County Library KidsPage
Multnomah County Library, Portland, Ore. Acc. 12 May 1998.
http://www.multnomah.lib.or.us/lib/kids/

> The KidsPage contains site for "pleasure" reference—reading, games, etc. Extensive, useful, and with a sense of immediacy to its community.

NassauNet's Kidspage, Nassau County Libraries
Nassau County Libraries, N.Y. Acc. 30 May 1998.
http://www.nassaulibrary.org/childrens/kidsmainpage.html

> Super Sites, Cool Sites, and Homework Help sections.

National Cathedral School Upper School Library Internet Database
National Cathedral School Upper School Library, Washington, D.C.
Acc. 12 May 1998.
http://www.ncs.cathedral.org/library/upper/ncsid/

> Searchable database and very clean layout marks this outstanding site.

Tennessee School for the Deaf
Marr Memorial Library. University of Tennessee, Knoxville, Tenn. Acc.
30 May 1998.
http://voyager.rtd.utk.edu/~tsd/library/library.html

> Nicely done page for Tennessee's deaf community.

What's Hot on the Internet This Week
El Dorado County Library, Placerville, Calif. Updated weekly. Acc. 12 May 1998.
http://www.el-dorado.ca.us/~lib-pl/thisweek.htm

> Another good idea for keeping a site current if you, your staff, or colleagues are prepared to watch for good sites.

Index

Walter Minkel is a youth librarian with more than twenty years' experience, a puppeteer, and a storyteller, but the Web lured him away. He is now School Corps Technology Trainer for Multnomah County (Oregon) Library. He manages the KidsPage for Multnomah County Library and created the Newbery and Caldecott Medal home pages and the Coretta Scott King Awards page for ALA. He is also comanager, with Roxanne Hsu Feldman, of the ALSC Web site. He has written several articles on young people and the Web for *School Library Journal.*

Roxanne Hsu Feldman is the senior middle school librarian at the Dalton School in New York City. She loves telling stories, sharing her love of books with children and seeing the sparks in children's eyes when they find something on the Web that excites them. When she worked at The New York Public Library she was involved in creating the "On-Lion" Web page for children. Roxanne (aka Fairrosa) is also the creator of the widely known Fairrosa Cyber Library on the Web.